Paul

Addicted to Wedding Cake

. . . the Journey of Divorce

I hope you enjoy

[signature]

By Keith G Churchouse © 2010

The Second Churchouse Chronicles©

First Edition

The first in the series of *Churchouse Chronicles*
is the book, ***Sign here, here and here!***
. . . Journey of a Financial Adviser

www.signherehereandhere.co.uk

Released March 2010

Available in paperback and e-reader ISBN: 978-0-9564325-0-6

ISBN 978-0-9564325-2-0

Further information, contact and order details can be found at: www.addictedtoweddingcake.co.uk

No financial advice of any description is offered or deemed to have been provided during the text of this book.

No legal advice is given or provided by this text and you should refer to your legal adviser for specific information about your needs and requirements.

The text refers to the divorce procedure of England and Wales. Other processes may be used in other parts of the UK.

Some of the names, titles, sequencing, areas and dates in this book have been amended to ensure that this work portrays a personal experience rather than those of individuals or companies. Any similarity to individuals or groups is purely coincidental.

This book is an expression of personal opinion of the author on his journey through divorce and its effects.

Churchouse is a Registered Trademark of Churchouse Financial Planning Limited.

The H.M Court Service forms contained within the text of this book have been reproduced with the kind authority and permission of HM Court Services.

A donation will be made to the charity *Association for Spina Bifida and Hydrocephalus* for each book sold.

Registered Charity No: 249338. *www.asbah.org*

Acknowledgements

Esther Dadswell

The first acknowledgement and thanks has to go to Esther, my wife, who has provided help and experience in the process of collating this text. Thank you also for staying around.

I would not have taken the best part of this journey without you. Your input has been invaluable.

My parents, Rosamund and Roger Churchouse

*Thank you for also putting up with me.
It's been fun, for me anyway!*

Thank you for standing by me to mop up the pieces after my life has been turned upside down by the effects of divorce, and for allowing me time to find myself and guiding me on how to start again.

You were right: there is life after divorce, although I did not see it so clearly at the time.

To the guiding hands that have helped me with this book

Thanks to:

Fiona Cowan, Words That Work,
contact: fifix@btopenworld.com

Graham Booth, Creation Booth,
contact: www.creationbooth.com

Jo Parfitt, Creative Mentor,
contact: www.joparfitt.com

Tom Evans, The Bookwright,
contact: www.thebookwright.com

To my learned friends

Thank you to Karin Walker and Kim Finnis, both
divorce lawyers of the highest calibre based in
Guildford, who have cast their learned eyes over
the text. Thank you for all of your help, support and
consideration. Their forewords follow.

Thank you also to Gordon Bowden, friend and fellow
financial planner, for his continued support and wisdom.

To my solicitors and barrister

Thanks for the invoices, all of them!

Accompanying website:

www.addictedtoweddingcake.co.uk

Forewords

By *Karin Walker*, Family Lawyer, Collaborative Lawyer and Mediator

Divorce is a process that one in three adults will experience – at least once. The circumstances surrounding a divorce or separation and the process itself can be one of the most traumatic endurances faced during adult life. Notwithstanding the prevalence of divorce, neutral, 'matter of fact', support is surprisingly not very readily available.

"*Addicted to Wedding Cake*" represents a layperson's practical guide to the pitfalls of this commonplace but traumatic process, written by someone who has experienced this process (more than once). Whilst no substitute for legal advice the book provides a step by step companion, in easily readable form, striking exactly the right balance between a light hearted approach and a concise road map through this serious topic.

As Keith details, each client will react differently to the divorce process and I am an advocate of discussing the options available at the outset to see which option, including the collaborative process, would best suit them.

Keith Churchouse is to be commended for clearly analysing his own experiences in a way that enables the reader to translate this into what is going on in their own life. And in Keith's own words "if, after reading about the process, the possible tribulations and cost in terms of time and money you decide to work harder at your marriage union, I will at least be able to say that I saved one marriage". Alternatively the "addiction to wedding cake" may continue . . .

Karin Walker

Family Lawyer, Collaborative Lawyer and Mediator
Principal, TWM Solicitors LLP, Guildford, Surrey
www.twmsolicitors.com

By Kim Finnis, Family Lawyer, Collaborative Lawyer and Mediator

Separation and divorce involve major life changes, which have a far reaching effect on future well-being and financial security for all involved. Whilst each separation or divorce is unique; it is certainly a time of considerable emotional turmoil. After death of a partner, divorce or separation is said to be the most stressful life event one can experience.

In *"Addicted to Wedding Cake"*, Keith addresses the process of divorce and its issues along the way. Having been through the process of divorce twice and having remarried, Keith draws on his own experience with a view to providing practical tips and guidance. There is a particularly helpful section on pensions - an area where Keith has considerable professional expertise.

Keith is ready to point out that using a specialist family lawyer is well worthwhile and this is commendable. Keith also deals with the alternatives to court that are available. For those looking to resolve matters constructively but who are not able to do this around the kitchen table, the options of the Collaborative approach, or mediation will be of interest.

Divorce and separation is a bewildering time. This is an easy to read book in an understandable format and an excellent lay person's guide for anyone approaching the subject. Well done Keith.

Kim Finnis,

Family Lawyer, Collaborative Lawyer and Mediator
Kim Finnis, Solicitor, Guildford, Surrey
www.kimfinnis.co.uk

Contents

Index page of divorce terms and phrases

Addicted to Wedding Cake . . . the Journey of Divorce

Once the divorce ball starts rolling, you will hear many terms and phrases (the jargon of the English and Welsh divorce world) that are likely to be unfamiliar to you. Unfortunately, some of these terms will become all too familiar as you go through the system.

To help understanding and to ease the process, I have listed below some of the terms and phrases that you may encounter in alphabetical order and referenced them to the pages on which they appear to help you navigate the terms as they arise in the context of the proceedings.

Introduction

The landing of my flight at JFK Airport was smooth enough, considering the rain storm that had lasted the whole of the night. In fact, the landing was in far better shape than the cab driver, who was late picking me up. I was not sure whether it was he or the luggage that was dragging the other across the cold and wet car park as I jumped into the black saloon that smelt of stale cigarettes, inadequately masked by cheap air freshener.

Most years in New York the traffic starts building up from immediately after Thanksgiving until Christmas, and today was no exception. An impromptu detour through a suburb failed to improve our average speed. As we approached a busy junction under a raised green underground gantry, through the rain-smeared window I noticed a placard advert strapped to a steel support: *Divorce only $299!* Fantastic! Can it be that easy and cheap? Sadly, the truth was hinted at by the listing underneath: *Bankruptcy $399!* It gave me the feeling that the offers were not unrelated, because if you used the first service you would need the second one shortly afterwards!

The reality is that this may not be the case and many separations and divorces are resolved in amicable and mature ways, resisting any urge or influence to fight about the outcome agreed. I am aware that this may not always be possible and that some conflict may ensue in proceeding through the divorce process in England and Wales. Divorce is also a journey and you will know that every journey you take is usually different. Divorce will also be a journey for you and the direction you take cannot be mapped, but the system or process used can be.

In reading this text, it would not be unreasonable to assume that you, the reader, are involved in the process of divorce somehow. This could be in a professional capacity, such as a legal adviser or mediator or, alternatively, because you have an enquiring mind about how the path of divorce may unravel in its journey. If you are about to start the divorce process or have recently entered this area of family law, I believe that these notes will at least manage some of your expectations of what hoops you will need to climb through to reach the legal separation that may seem so far away at this point.

Personally, I have been married three times and divorced twice. It's advisable to keep these things legal, and the bigamy rules are pretty stiff in the UK! Bearing in mind that these depressing accolades had already been achieved by the grand old age of 37, you can work out that I am a 'high mileage' person. I am not proud of the errors of my ways . . . or were they just the pressures of life? And you must also remember that I am a man, viewing this subject from a man's point of view, however careful I have been to provide balanced comment.

For many people, this track record will look like a lifetime's worth of marriages and divorces, crammed into less than a decade. These personal changes can prove to be a valuable experience, if only to force you to define what really matters to you. I have worked in financial services for 25 years and am qualified (by examination and experience) to provide financial advice in divorce situations. That sums up my knowledge and (sadly) experience to enable me to write this book.

These are notes from some of my memories, learning and experiences through the maze that is divorce. You may well see this maze from the day the rug gets pulled from under your feet, to the day you marry again, and all the way back again, if that happens to you. Finally, one day in the future, peace returns to everyone's shattered lives and you will find you can truly breathe again.

My wife Esther (and yes, I am happily married again) suggested recently that for her, getting divorced was like, 'jumping off a cliff with a blindfold on. You know you're going to hit the ground hard; it's just a question of which outcrops you hit on the way down and no one tells you how deep the drop is.' Then she added with a smile of irony, 'and there's no peeking from under the blindfold!' I am very grateful to Esther for sharing with me some of her feelings about her experiences during her divorce. This has enabled me to bring some well needed female perspective and balance to this book.

You may have already fitted your blindfold for the leap you are about to take from your marriage? And if so, then you need to recognise that you may well already have had a 'jump moment' in your marriage. If this book helps you with your decision making process, it will have fulfilled a good part of its purpose. After reading about the process, the possible tribulations and costs, in terms of time and money, you decide to work harder at your marriage union, I will at least be able to then say that I saved one marriage.

How right Esther's comments are and for many this is the case. From my own experience each divorce is unique and presents its own difficulties. We are all unique and so are the circumstances, beliefs, standards, ages and ethics that will carve or mould the final financial settlement and *Decree Absolute* that may be finally celebrated with a glass of wine in some months' or even years' time.

Don't worry about understanding these divorce terms, such as *Decree Absolute*, at this stage because all will become clear as we proceed through the forthcoming pages. For ease, I have also included an Index of Divorce Terms page (page 16, above) which gives the terms and phrases (jargon). You may wish to use this as a 'ready reckoner' to try and cut through some of the jargon that your legal adviser may use when discussing your case.

Esther, likes to joke that I must be *'addicted to wedding cake'*, based on the number of times that I have been married. I am pleased to say that some years after my last divorce, I am able to engage in this witty banter with her without feeling aggrieved at being the target of such jollity. Personally, I do have to be light-hearted at the situation of having clocked up three marriages and two divorces, because if you don't then it can take you to dark chasms of gloom that you would visit only out of necessity. However, divorce creates that necessity sometimes, especially when the process turns personal and this can then lead (in my opinion) to a theft of some dignity, which can happen.

Also, the title of *'Addicted to Wedding Cake'* may leave you wondering if I am a large man, with a fetish for all things iced, or a marzipan muncher. This is not the case, although on those nauseating medical charts that the doctors keep forcing upon the great and the good of the

UK, I do come under the heading of 'obese' — but these days, doesn't everyone? I will touch on the subject of keeping fit during the divorce process later in the book. It also leaves the door wide open to jokes comparing a person's husband or wife to the cake that was used to celebrate the union, such as a 'fruitcake', a 'sponge' or just plain 'nutty'. Let me assure you that this book is not going to be a trip into the 'bitter barn'. Apart from such a temptation being puerile, the details of the court proceedings in Family Law are confidential; this makes it improper to divulge some specifics.

During the book I will talk about some of the emotive stages that you may experience during the divorce process. Dependent on where you are in the process may affect which part of the book you may want to reference. If you are at the initial and possibly angry phase and looking for signposting of the proceedings, you may want to skip straight to chapters 2 and 3 to look at the divorce process and the paperwork involved. On the other hand, if you are further into the process or considering your options, then you may find this introduction and later chapters a good read.

Also, don't forget that your close family and friends may want to understand what you are going through in your divorce and where you are up to. They might want to see this book to help their understanding. They were probably there to celebrate the original union and hopefully you will remember what that meant to you and why you tied the knot in the first place.

What are the institutions of marriage and family?

What does the institution of marriage mean to you? Exactly what does a standard family look like? What is considered normal anyway? And does it matter to you or your spouse?

I remember growing up in a happy household in the 1960's and 1970's. There were two parents pushing me on, two siblings to play with and a Ford on the driveway. Many people would argue that this was the perfect nuclear family.

In the twenty-first century, there no longer seems to be an agreed definition of the standard family. I am not sure one exists any more. Does this matter? With 'guest parents' in many households, step-children and grand parents, the boundaries we once knew and to some extent enjoyed now seem a distant memory. The 'family issue' and the demise of its boundaries have proved an excellent political football for our MPs to kick around and moralise about for years to come.

But overall, marriage is what both you and your spouse make it. Only you can decide the shape of this. Only you can decide if it works for you, your marriage and your family.

Where does it all change?

It may be from our twenties that life goes from fun to serious? You change from being a 'taker' at the beginning of your decade, frolicking around and having fun, to a 'provider', mortgaged to the highest level that you can afford, possibly with children, a promotion to work towards and an expanding waistline? Or is it the thirties? Whichever it is for you, you will start to recognise the routine.

And what of your partner? How are they coping with the change that is called modern life? How is he or she coping with his or her chosen partner, namely *you*?

At these ages you also usually start to have confidence in who you are and what you aspire to. Your friends and contacts change and the pressures of family life and work start to control your diary, both socially and in business.

Then, having settled down with a long term partner, the inevitable time arrives when you have to make a decision about what you are going to do about your future together, such as marriage. Or you may have the attitude of being relaxed with each other about your long term futures and not need to go through this ceremony.

This is not the case for most of us, and it could be for various reasons. You might be ready for the 'C' word (Commitment); or there might be other reasons, such as a biological clock ticking. But you will only know the final reason when the day comes. Whatever it is, you wake up one morning single and go to bed in the evening engaged.

Fruitcake anyone?

It is likely that the initial engagement announcement will generate excitement from friends, family and colleagues at the start of the 'Big Day' planning frenzy. This will also usually generate the beginning of the vast expense and family bickering about how the 'Big Day' is going to unfurl.

In this modern consumer-driven world, it is too easy to get sucked into the 'wedding machine' that guides you towards how other people want to spend your money, rather than what the couple themselves want from their blessing, party or even wedding cake.

'Now remember, the bride's mother has the first choice of colour of her outfit and the groom's mother cannot clash with that, so this needs to be managed . . .' you get the picture. You as a modern couple also probably get the bulk of the expense as well.

Knowing your partner as you do, you are likely to know what he or she will want to get out of the day. It is up to you to anticipate and respect this, to keep any friction to a minimum. This may mean that you have to pay for the event — but it is the strings that come with financial offers of help that you have to watch out for.

Although terribly unromantic, now might also be a time to at least consider taking specialist legal advice about the option of entering into a pre-nuptial agreement. I understand the courts are giving these more consideration and the law may be in a process of change in this area.

Esther advises me that many women form an opinion at an early age as to what their perfect wedding outfit and event will look like on their 'Big Day'. Most people only plan to marry once so, so the plans for the day have to be perfect. Once you understand that, you understand the importance of getting it right. For Esther and I it was a simple service, bearing in mind that we were already 'high mileage' by the time we got to the registry office, and my finest Levi jeans were the order of the day, although I must admit Esther's dress was excellent.

Honeymoons

An excellent way of demonstrating how the world has changed and become a smaller place in our modern world is the way we travel around it.

Honeymoons show how many newlyweds (along with other travellers) now reach the four corners of the world as a matter of course, almost the norm, rather than Bognor Regis for a long weekend, as achieved by many couples fifty years ago. Thinking about one honeymoon, this was two weeks in an all-inclusive resort, drinking much of the local brew and enjoying the sunshine. This was my first trip to the Caribbean and was expensive at the time. I have been there many times since and I think the total cost of these trips has been similar to the cost of that first one on its own.

Honeymoons are also a strange experience as they are the beginning of the end of the celebrations of the union . . . and the beginning of the marriage and married life. Many couples who were already living together see this as a normal holiday with a bit of a 'do' beforehand. Some couples will hold another party when they get home, to accommodate friends and family who could not make the main event. For others, this is a once in a lifetime experience to be savoured; and rightly so.

There are people on their second or third honeymoon, usually trying something completely new in line with the newly restored lease of life that they are now experiencing after a divorce and the 'release' from a previous marriage. Many feel that there is some living to be caught up with.

This can be evidenced by the growing number of divorcees over the age of fifty. They have spent the first phase of adult life with their spouse and achieved many goals in their lives, such as children, a family home and possibly their own business. But, having achieved the first chapters of their lives, they decide, either mutually or individually, and possibly with the children having left home, that they would like to undertake a different future alone or with someone else.

Some would argue that this is because they have another phase of their life ahead and want to try something completely new and independent. Possibly there is an element of the grass appearing 'greener' on the other side of the fence, and with the possibility of greater longevity, they feel they have time to do it.

Many of the over-fifties are 'baby boomers' who have enjoyed the benefit of final salary pension schemes and house price inflation over their lifetimes, leaving them with a good standard of living, even after a divorce. Their decision to divorce (at any age) is their decision — and some live to regret it. This is because they find that they miss their friend of the last twenty or thirty years, rather than their ex-spouse.

As I am sure you will remember, although the 'Big Day' is very special and you are confirming your commitment to your partner, you may well be back at work three weeks later and still wanting to undertake the hobbies that you enjoyed before the marriage — those hobbies that hopefully your partner bought into before and when he or she said 'Yes!' to that romantic proposal you made.

Toys!

To some extent, we all need our own hobbies and hobby 'toys' and somewhere to play with them. A bit of 'you' time, although I am not sure why. This certainly seems to be the case for both men and women. The hobbies of each sex may require a different environment, cost and time requirement to achieve fulfilment. I am sure that some boffin can trace the source of this desire back to a Neanderthal 'being' and their cave habits of making tools or fire to kill and cook animals. However, I am sure the same boffins are unable to note that said Neanderthal being had a family to care for who issued them with a list of grocery requirements for the week and kicked them out of the cave with the shout: 'And don't come back unless you have got me a juicy mammoth or sabre tooth tiger!'

No, each person is different and each of their hobbies will have different 'toy' requirements.

As examples, (and I concur with those that the next part might be a male centric approach to the subject) the male of the household might be modern gadget man, or garden man, a DIY-er or a model maker, music man, petrol head… However, you should also remember that for some people, men and women, work is their sole motivation. This might be because it is their own business which will not function without them at the helm (or so they believe!). Or perhaps they are on a graduate programme to the top and nothing is going to stand in the way of their success, not even their marriage.

And each hobby will need an environment to enjoy the pastime. This might be in the form of a club, shed, garage, gym, coffee shop, music room, a spare room, a den, or for those in business, their office or business premises. Many people find that the routine of business life is a comforting factor, especially when their home life starts to crumble. If you can't recognise yourself in at least one of these categories, then I suggest that you get out a little more.

I'm just the same. I am 'Mr Petrol Head' and my garage is my 'den' — preferably stuffed to the rafters with as many petrol engine 'toys' as I can cram in there. By 'toys', I mean the latest petrol driven gadget that can trim the hedge or cut the lawn, or do 70 miles per hour (honest, officer!) on two wheels down the local bypass. For others it might be a collection of computer technology or a football strip for their favourite team.

A man planning to get married has to decide what he wants to do with his toy collection. In the case of cars and motorcycles, does he want to drive them, or polish them, or dismantle them and rebuild them as a project, or will he be content just to know that they are under his ownership? And how will that 'toy' or 'den' decision be affected by the marriage, his spouse's views, or as another example, the patter of tiny feet and their effects on the family budget?

I realise that these last paragraphs possibly make us chaps out to be rather a self-centred bunch. However, whatever form your hobby takes, toys and somewhere to play with them are essential to many people's well being.

I think it also helps both parties tie into their joint life. As an example, a wife might know that her husband is tinkering/listening/building in the shed/garage/study rather than up to no good in the local pub or worse. And these pastimes are there to be shared and enjoyed together, although I am aware that many women would rather have nothing to do with their man's pastime; sharing the occasional cup of tea in the shed may be the most you can hope for!

Never forget that if you ask your spouse to endure too much, this alone can be cited as your unreasonable behaviour in the divorce Petition served against you. It does not have to be proved, but it can make you feel uncomfortable because you'd naively thought that nobody including your spouse minded your little pastime.

This could lead to the question of what you did want to achieve from your marriage and if this objective has changed?

Love leaves the room when the money runs out!

Because divorce proceedings expose the private goings-on between two parties, the details are usually shielded from public view by all parties involved and this is why so many people are surprised by the invasive nature of what really goes on in the process when it happens to them.

Divorce is a personal litigation against your spouse, to untie yourself (and your money) from the union of the contract established at the time you took your vows. It may be because the love you once shared for each other has died or, as another example, that the money has run out and things have become difficult. Whatever the reason, you may find that when the budget strings that you had both mutually and willingly allowed to become untied now tighten, all attitudes to putting up with each other and the various foibles can change quickly.

As an end to this introduction, many will realise divorce is an emotionally charged time for all participants (willing or not), which is sometimes not recognised by the well qualified advisers that provide you with guidance, but have never experienced the process at first hand. This may make some individuals appear to be unconnected to your concerns and sometimes make you feel that you have not communicated clearly. This can cause many hours of frustration and if you pursue this frustration, you may see your costs rise (they rarely fall!) as you seek to score or express a point that is of limited value in the bigger picture that is your future life.

However, help is at hand in the divorce process through new initiatives using a collaborative process, first used in America and now being successfully employed in England and Wales. This is an excellent alternative and is detailed further in the book.

Dressed to kill

For many people, the start of a divorce is a difficult and troubling time, but also a time of great release. For some people, it is a time to buy a new wardrobe, usually everything that the other half hated, and to flaunt their attributes, whether they are male or female, often in front of the soon to be ex-spouse as often as possible. You might see this as the *I didn't need you anyway* effect. I am sure someone will make a perfume called that one day.

Jesting apart, be ready for this consequence as it could be a tactic designed to make you regret your decision or your apathy towards the relationship that you once enjoyed.

Dark humour and history

Divorce can be a heavy subject and one that many happily married people choose to ignore. This leaves many of us uninformed of the overall process until, one day, suddenly we need to know everything all at once.

This book is designed to be a positive learning experience about what the process might look like with a few smiles thrown in. I will note this for you early in the text, you *will* survive and thrive after the process, it just that at this point, the start of the process, you may not feel that this is possible.

Divorce is nothing new and has been highly prevalent in England and Wales for many decades. Who can forget Henry the Eighth?

Some people would prefer not to be seen reading this little book as it may send the wrong message. It will be interesting to see if we sell more copies of this text as an e-reader, to allow those with an interest in the subject the freedom to read the text from an electronic and discreet screen without fear of being noticed.

Notes/ Questions to ask?

Notes/ Questions to ask?

1. What is divorce?

Have you ever really asked yourself: 'what is this divorce thing about?' You may never have to consider this question. You might be one of the fortunate couples who make it to the end of their lives without a *Decree Absolute*. (That's a divorce to you and me.)

However, if you're in the varying and large category of marriages and couples who do not make it to their final resting place in blissful harmony, then this book might be for you in understanding the process, money, consequences and life after the divorce. It will certainly help to manage your expectations.

You might guess that I have made more than a few notes from personal experience. You may want to call me a 'divorce junkie' if you like, but I do hope that I have given up the divorce habit now. The good news is that statistics released in 2010 by the Office for National Statistics show that divorce in England and Wales is at a 29 year low.

As with any statistics, you can draw your own conclusions. This statistic above may mean that either we are all a lot more content with our married lives or chosen spouse or, alternatively, that we can't afford a solicitor yet to get a divorce because of the economic climate or the equity value in the matrimonial home for example?

This raises the question of what divorce is about? Surely getting divorced is not that difficult or expensive. Or is it?

One definition of divorce is: *a judicial declaration dissolving a marriage in whole or in part, esp. one that releases the husband and wife from all matrimonial obligations* (source: www.dictionary.com).

Thinking about your own situation, if you are in or about to start your divorce journey you may like to ask yourself the following questions:

- Did you jump or did you fall into it?

- Did you get pushed or did you launch yourself freely into the abyss of divorce, possibly with even more eagerness than you had when embarking on the marriage all that time ago?

I have mentioned my wife, Esther, in the introduction of this book. Esther has helped me with the content and I am relieved that the balance that she has brought to the text ensures that I stay on the right side of avoiding many male chauvinist comments that are neither constructive, nor helpful.

At the start of the divorce process, you may be unaware of any discontent within your household. You won't have noticed any change, such as your better half packing an 'emotional parachute' for that big 'jump', possibly while you're not paying full attention. You may have no clue about the destruction about to wreak havoc in your domestic life or, if you are the orchestrator, the disappointment that you are about to bring home. You may need a ready reckoner on how this is going to work out — and you've come to the right place.

Welcome to the hallowed and hollow institution that is divorce. In my experience, nothing can really prepare you for divorce, even if you are the one that initiates the process, usually noted by the physical action of leaving. Hopefully you are only going to go through this system once, if at all. As Esther comments in the introduction, this book aims to help you with the bumps you should expect on the way down. Therefore, some people might see this book as an 'emotional parachute' on the way to their final destination.

The path mapped here will be relevant whether you are the one doing the jumping or the pushing, I shall refer to you as the 'jumpers' during the course of this text, rather than the term that your ex or soon to be ex-spouse uses for you. I'm sure you know which expletive that may be if they are of that nature.

If you have been divorced in the past (and one in five divorcing have been (source: Office of National Statistics/ www.ons.gov.uk/2008)) or are only now thinking about starting the process for the first time, you will know exactly which day and can probably pinpoint the very moment when the thought *'I am not doing this anymore'* first appeared as a 'bubble' in your scrambled mind. This is the point where you have forgiven them this, forgiven them that and then a final *'forget it'* pops into your head after too many past transgressions become unforgivable.

I also say *'scrambled mind'* because for many people divorce is a time of turmoil. It certainly was for me and in different ways for each divorce situation. You may well be uncertain as to which direction you are heading, although usually the only certainty you may have is that as long as this chosen direction is away from your spouse then that is fine.

The exit of separation, it transpires, can be like jumping off a cliff. For others, the decision is clear cut, almost clinical in its execution, where the thought of leaving and final decision are one — a trial, judgement and executioner all in one! Maybe this type of positive decision-making was the thing that made the two parties attractive to each other in the first place. And now, it is the same type of decision-making that will take them apart.

For other people it is less clear cut. They experience a gentle waning of the love and affection that they jointly nurtured all those years ago, possibly before children and mortgages came along to occupy minds and distance the partners from the personal values which they once held true. You might wake up one day next to the person that you have lain with for decades and realise that you don't know them anymore. You may even realise that you do not like them either. Personally, I don't think this is anyone's fault, although the modern world loves to make a villain and victim out of such situation and this may well always be the case.

In this chapter I have mentioned in the text some selected points from the Office of National Statistics, and as you will see there are more to come. As already noted, you can deduce what you want from statistics. However, their website makes for interesting reading even if it is to prove one thing. That you are not alone in going through the divorce journey, with tens of thousands in the process at any one time, affecting families, individuals and households all over England and Wales.

Statistics, statistics, statistics

That last paragraph or two may seem a bit cynical, as though I were suggesting that every marriage is doomed and this is certainly not the case. However, the reality of the situation is demonstrated in the following statistics from the Office of National Statistics for 2008:

The total number of divorces granted in England and Wales in 2008 was 121,779. This was a fall of 5.0 per cent, and the lowest figure since around 1976, the year of punks and the long hot summer, if you remember those days. The peak year for divorce was in 2003 at 153,176.

Here are some statistics in 2008:

- 67 per cent of divorces in England and Wales in 2008 were awarded to the wife

- The average age of a man at divorce in 2008 was 43.9, and for a woman 41.4 years

- The average marriage in 2008 lasted 11.5 years (that's a 12-year itch, so stop scratching!)

- One in five men and women divorcing in 2008 had a previous marriage ending in divorce

- For all divorces granted to an individual (rather than to both) behaviour was the most common factor in the breakup

- The age group with the highest divorce rate is people in their late twenties

(Source: Office of National Statistics Online, www.ons.gov.uk)

There are many more statistics on this website. As noted in some of the information above, many of the results make interesting reading, including the number of younger children involved in the marriages that are dissolved.

Stigma

There is still some social stigma attached to the institution of divorce, but you will get over this quickly. In legal terms you are petitioning someone, or being petitioned, for the end of a marriage contract and your case will be presented before a judge to be approved. A dictionary definition of *Petition* is 'ask humbly'. Should you be the *Petitioner* (the person bringing the proceedings into a court of law) you may not be asking so humbly.

When you are divorcing someone, say on the grounds of their Adultery or Unreasonable Behaviour, you are the 'Petitioner' and the other side responds back to your Petition. This means that the other person becomes the 'Respondent' (one who answers). You will soon get to know these terms and as noted, they are detailed in the Index page. Some parties in a divorce like to be noted as the 'Petitioner' because they feel that it implies they have the moral high ground. This is because they had grounds to Petition the Respondent for their deeds of wrong doing. Don't get too hung up on this point, it does not help and may be costly if disputed. The 'grounds' for divorce are detailed further in Chapter 2.

Once the 'divorce' ball starts to roll, it is likely that it will only stop when the process has finished. Rarely are there any real reconciliations. Many people around you will 'hold court' over your circumstances and make up their own minds about who are the guilty and aggrieved parties, and sentence each incumbent accordingly. At the end of this book, I'm sure you will do the same thing by making a judgement on its content and the experiences I have shared. This is only natural. As you will see later in this book, this 'judging' behaviour can be fascinating, and usually for the wrong reasons.

Your legal adviser or solicitor will guide you through the divorce process and use their understanding of family law to negotiate a financial settlement and legal separation for you. That's what you pay them for. The law and its judgements evolve through time, as with any people-focused profession. Divorce is all about people and their lives, both past and present. As you know, no two people are the same and those people's lives evolve and change. While this evolution is taking place, we will naturally notice some changes.

A good example of this type of evolution can be evidenced by official court forms illustrated in this book and used for divorce. These are due to change in or around the next year or so. I would recommend that you view the website www.hmcs.gov.uk to keep updated. This is the website of Her Majesty's Court Service (HMCS) and you may need to know whether any of the divorce forms replicated here with their kind permission have changed or been updated. You will want to keep focused on being up to date to ensure that you don't waste time filling in the wrong forms, although your legal adviser should guide you on these documents accordingly.

Don't be under any illusion that things won't get complicated. They may well do, especially if you have financial assets such as shares, your own company or a final salary pension scheme. Other professionals, such as Actuaries, Valuers and Pension Advisers, may need to be involved to allow you to complete your court submission, such as your Financial Disclosure Form (Form E), if you use one.

The largest of these forms is called a Form E, which acts as a financial fact-find, illustrated later in Appendix 1, and gives a guide as to the depth of the information that you may be required to submit to court. Bear in mind, this *is* a court submission, so no fibbing is allowed. You may find yourself burrowing into the mire if any details you chose to leave off are exposed in the course of a divorce hearing. Remember, deliberately leaving information off is perjury and not recommended. Also, remember that this is also the case for your soon to be ex-partner.

You may agree in your negotiations that you do not need to complete a Form E, however many still do and a financial statement and exchange of information will certainly be required.

Nothing new?

Divorce seems to be quite a modern but nevertheless historic British institution, with some of the highest divorce rates in Europe for 50 years dating from the 1960s (source: Office of National Statistics). As examples, the number of divorces granted in England and Wales in 1961 was approximately 27,000, rising to 56,000 by 1969, and then doubling to around 125,000 divorces by 1972.

Some have argued and research does back up that this followed the social revolution in the UK in the early 1960s, which among other things generated more liberal attitudes to sex, promiscuity, marriage and divorce. It is strange to think that part of the divorce culture in England and many other countries started after the Second World War. Returning soldiers, sailors and airmen came home from the war to new domestic circumstances and a spouse who had changed because of the effects of the war. Some decided that they wanted to move on to something different.

The Government and authorities of the time noted this change and tried to persuade couples that marriage was no longer the institution it once was, but a relationship shared between two people. However, the new freedom of the 1960s and 1970s saw the divorce rate increase significantly in 1971-1972. This followed the Divorce Reform Act (1969). Some see the Act as opening the floodgates, changing the law and now allowing divorce on five grounds, three of which (Adultery, Unreasonable behaviour (originally cruelty) and Desertion) were deemed to be 'faults', to which the 'aggrieved' spouse can apply for divorce proceedings.

The two other grounds were seen as 'non fault'. The full details of these grounds are detailed later in the text at Chapter 2 and are covered at length in the process section. The 1969 Divorce Reform Act was replaced in 1996 by the Family Law Act. The Statute governing divorce is the Matrimonial Causes Act 1973, as amended.

This history provides us with more insight into divorce in England and Wales, a phenomenon, which has been highly prevalent in our environment for around half a century.

Irony

To live is to experience change, both in yourself and in your partner or partners throughout your time on this planet. The saying goes that *life begins at forty*. This was probably true in the 1960s and 1970s because, based on normal life expectancy, you could confidently expect to live to around the age of 75. Based on this statistic, at around 40 years old you were halfway through your life. Many people thought it was a good time to shake things up in some way, and for some this was the beginning of their mid-life crisis.

However, modern studies suggest that now only around ten per cent of adults still suffer a mid-life crisis. This is because an individual's expectation of health, prospects and life expectancy have now been extended significantly by healthier lifestyles, advances in medicines and a wealthier modern lifestyle. With this new generic affluence in midlife comes a reduced desire to make sudden changes, such as divorce.

Life for many of us has changed and prospects for many individuals seem better in most arenas, such as health, employment and longevity. If you are on the receiving end of an unwelcome divorce Petition then you can take some solace from the fact that time may well be on your side to start another phase in your life, which might not have been the case had you reached your mid-life thirty or forty years earlier, such as the 1950s and 1960s.

Notes/ Questions to ask?

Notes/ Questions to ask?

2. The divorce process

Some may argue that this part of the book is what you have been waiting for, almost the 'nitty gritty' of the divorce process. From the day you decide to part in yourself to starting again will be detailed in the next few chapters.

The paper chase begins

One of the first things I would recommend is that you might want to think about buying a lever arch file to store all of the papers, letters and correspondence that will start once the divorce ball is rolling.

Why do solicitors' letters seem only ever to arrive on a Saturday morning? They hit your doormat just in time to ruin the latest of your rather average weekends alone since the divorce process started. You have little money with which to enjoy yourself because it is being spent on the invoice that came with the letter explaining that financially things had just got a lot worse, for some new reason.

You then have the rest of the weekend to stew over what on earth is going on. . . before you can speak to your solicitor on the Monday morning, having wound yourself up for 36 hours or so. I did warn you!

When you get divorced, there are various elements to the process.

From a legal point of view, to achieve a divorce, you require a *Decree Nisi* first and, subsequently, a *Decree Absolute*. The only grounds for divorce are the irretrievable breakdown of the marriage. These *grounds* are evidenced by one of the five 'facts' of divorce, which are Adultery, Unreasonable Behaviour, Desertion, Two year separation (with consent) and Five year separation. I have detailed these further in Section g, later.

The *Decree Absolute* is the document that dissolves your marriage and permits you to marry again, if you have not had enough the first time round. If there was no money involved and the courts of England and Wales were not overburdened with applications to divorce, then I understand that both documents could be organised in around four months. However, there is that tricky bit in the middle, and it's called *money*. Most divorce participants would not want to agree to a *Decree Absolute* until a *Financial Settlement or Order* is legally agreed. Any applicant taking advice from a good solicitor usually wouldn't.

Divorce will take time, money and energy. The next part of the book puts the process of divorce into some order. This does not mean that your divorce will follow this process and in the order detailed here, but this will give a reasonable guide/example as to how the process may look for your situation.

The outline of the divorce process:

- Deciding to part

- Identifying the opportunity to get out, both physically and financially

- Breaking the news and taking the leap

- Getting your soon to be ex-partner to understand that it really is over and you want a divorce

- Stating the reason for the divorce

- Instructing solicitors and the first letters

- Opening negotiations: who is keeping what and when and, in some cases most importantly, how?

- All parties agreeing an outline structure/solution of the financial separation

- Caring for and spending time with your children

- *Decree Nisi, Financial Settlement* and *Decree Absolute*

- Recovery

- Starting again

As noted before, your divorce may not follow these steps, it may well turn in different ways. Be prepared, the time gaps between each section may be a matter of hours, days, weeks or months. Each case is different and yours will be no exception.

Before we go any further, we should set some expectations on timing. The divorce process can be quite voluminous and time consuming with many areas to cover, but it is not difficult to understand, however acceptable or unacceptable it may seem. However, the time you must spend enduring the process, possibly many months, may not be acceptable, but unavoidable.

Stand and deliver . . . the time ticks by

This is not a reference to the catchy tune by Adam and the Ants, but to the time and cost that the divorce process can take. Many people see divorce as highway robbery, in terms of both time and cost, even if it is not. Remember that both are being spent during the process of legal separation.

If your particular indiscretion that has caused your divorce has, as an example, been Adultery and you imagine you can whisk your new found love up the aisle in a June wedding, then please feel free to plan ahead. Just don't fix which year because a divorce takes time.

As noted before, taking into account that most courts have a significant level of divorce applications, their ability to implement a quick turnaround is limited. Even if both parties are fully amicable to the divorce process, and can agree financial terms together over a glass of wine one evening (and yes, these people do exist) the legal process may slow their aspirations to go their separate ways legally.

In truth, for the average person on the omnibus of life, you are looking at around six to twelve months for a quick *Decree Absolute* and one to two years for the average process to grind through.

Counselling

Some people recommend counselling to help a marriage through a difficult patch. Even the most successful marriages have their tricky moments and, if needed, a few counselling sessions may be enough to get you back on track or to be reconciled if the difficulties have got that far. If you do not believe that your own marital problem has gone too far to retrieve, then try counselling. Together you may be a lot better for it. Working at a marriage is important and counselling can be part of that process. As an addition to this comment, it may only be one of you that seeks counselling and this can have significant personal benefits, particularly if you have started what for many is the lonely road of divorce.

I would add that if you have children or other dependants, counselling may also allow you both to learn to live with the idea that things are *not* going to work out, to understand why, and to know how to work together for the benefit of the family that you will both still love. I recommend Relate, a charity who offer a comprehensive service in these and many other family based circumstances. They have a national network of facilities available and their website is www.relate.org.uk. If there is no service locally then you may wish to try the Citizens Advice Bureau for further guidance. Their contact details can be found at: www.citizensadvice.org.uk

For many other people, counselling will not be the solution.

In some ways, it is a relief to know deep down that the union is over. It is the start of the process of solving the problem. The reality is that if you stay in your marriage then you may be living a lie. If you are prepared to do that, you need to understand that you are only burning away your own lifetime; the final cost will be far greater than the money that you could lose otherwise. Remember my comment earlier in this chapter about spending both money and time.

It comes as a shock to many people outside the marriage when they find out what is happening. However, it may have been obvious to you as part of the marriage for months, or even years.

The crime of being nice

Everyone has heard of *killing with kindness*. This can often be the case in marriages. I have heard of partners coming home to a 'Dear John' (*sorry I had to leave*) letter from their spouse to say that they could not stay because the person they lived with was *too nice, with the effect of smothering them.*

Marriage is about balance between two parties. When one of you tries *too* hard, even this can overwhelm the party that they love, smothering them in love and kindness that is just too much.

a. Deciding to part

No one can prepare you for the day when you or your spouse finally decide that it is over, the day he or she snaps and says 'it's over!', hits the wall — whatever you want to call it.

As suggested in the introduction to this book, this will be the day when you suddenly recognise that you are 'not doing this anymore!' You wake up one morning unhappily married and go to sleep that night in the spare room mentally separated and probably exhausted.

Some people find this a relief. Others may take weeks or even years to figure out why they have taken a wrong turn in their lives and to recognise that the only way out is to hit the divorce switch. Whether you are the 'pushed person' or the 'jumper', the writing is usually on the wall for a period of time before this day finally arrives.

The implosion may be rapid, with the occurrence of an infidelity, or one party suddenly leaving, or it may be that both parties admit the union is over and it is time to move on with no hope of reconciliation. These can be and usually are emotive times. At this point, there has to be an introduction to the mechanics of divorce.

The separation and divorce of a couple, I feel, has a lot to do with the ethics and values of each party. While you are still together you will usually share and respect these marital values, but as your union goes downhill the boundaries of these ethics are eroded until certain barriers are broken irrevocably.

An obvious crossing of a personal value could be Adultery, whereas the wronged spouse had quite fairly anticipated a monogamous relationship. Other boundaries might be the interference of relatives, or out of control spending by one partner. The list could go on but the fact is, when your own personal boundary is crossed, it may immediately put the marriage on a difficult course.

And please don't kid yourself that each of you doesn't know where these boundaries are. I am sure that a partner may plan to explain away the *indiscretion* that flies in the face of the cornerstone ethics that you had both adhered to, and then will probably repeat the same offence some time later. When a partner does that within your marriage, you will know it is time to go.

The Marriage Certificate that may break up the marriage

Some people live and thrive together for years without getting married and have very happy lives. However, there are some who decide after a long period of partnership that it is time to get married.

The reason for the decision to make it 'official' may not be logical, one-sided or even sensible. Many would argue that love is blind. However, for whatever reason the decision to marry is taken, it may be a poor decision if everything has worked well in the past for a long time. You will be aware that it does take a marriage certificate to provide each partner with financial security in the event of a separation and divorce. Although often referred to, there is no such thing as a common law wife or husband and also no protection.

Cabin fever

Many long term couples marry and then find that for some reason (and possibly the 'pressure' of a marriage certificate) they are tipped 'over the edge' and this eventually leads them to divorce. If this could be you, then think carefully about why you are taking the plunge after all this time. You do not want to regret your decision later.

I recently went on holiday, taking a cruise ship to the sunshine. I could not wait to get off the boat, but could not really put my finger on why. The cabin was well appointed, the food delicious, the weather good and the facilities just fine. So why did I nearly jump off the side of the boat at the first sight of land? I had heard the term *cabin fever* before, but I had never really understood what it was until I had been on board for a few days. There was really nothing wrong and you had full access to the whole ship; it was just the thought of being *confined* that drove me up the wall.

It appears that I was not alone. Many people feel this way. It occurs to me that for some people, the same claustrophobic experience happens in a marriage, with divorce to them being the first sighting of land and then jumping overboard. Anything can trigger this.

Esther jokes that she is the only one of my spouses not to have taken my name on marriage. But she feels that unknowingly this is important to me because it keeps me happier in myself. I cannot say for sure that this is true but there might be something in it.

As a rather harsh joke, Esther also goes on to remind me that it will work out cheaper to administer if we ever divorce!

b. Identifying the opportunity to separate

If you are the 'jumper' then you will start to consider packing your emotional parachute ready for when the day comes.

You will have been through a thousand times the thought process of why the division is approaching. You (along with your spouse) may have seen this coming for a long time. It may almost have become a natural evolution of the end of that union. No matter why you find yourself in this situation, preparation is the key to a smooth transition for all parties. This may seem a strange statement, but the care of all parties is paramount, however much you wish to be away from your spouse at that particular point for whatever marital crime they may have committed.

A mature attitude is the key.

Your spouse or family will still need you to provide for them and you need to build this into your divorce financial planning. If you have children, they are going to need to live with one of their parents and still see the other during the week or at weekends, with the relevant accommodation at both venues. They still need to be kept safe, warm and fed. You are still going to need to be clean, healthy and competent to fulfil your role as a parent.

So, where are you going to stay? How much is that going to cost? How long are you going to stay there? Can you afford it? Can you not *afford* to take the jump?

All of the above are difficult questions. However, with a bit of thought, planning and application it is amazing what can be achieved for the benefit of all parties. If you are going to take out a property tenancy agreement, then this is usually for a minimum period of six months, so you will need to budget for a six to twelve-month period. The letting agent will undertake a credit check (this is important and I have expanded on this subject in Section c), and will write to your employer or accountant if your self employed for a reference (you may want to warn them or those who may be involved in providing this information that a request is on its way before they get it. You may have already had to advise them of your situation if you have had to change home address quickly) and an electoral roll check. They will usually require four to six weeks rent as a deposit and one month's rent in advance. You can do the maths for the new home you are looking at.

I will mention this later, but please bear in mind that your solicitor is likely to want some money on account at the outset of your instructions and will need to see some identification for their records. You may want to keep these documents, such as passport, driving licence, birth certificate and so on, safe anyway, so make sure you take them with you at the time of the separation.

This may mean that correspondence will come to your matrimonial home address, so be ready and control this issue.

Many solicitors will cover this correspondence point with you at the outset to make sure that any mail is not inadvertently sent to a location to which an early warning of your next intentions can be given to the other party. You may want to arrange an alternative postal address in advance to cater for this issue, say a friend or relative whom you trust.

c. Breaking the news and making your move

This may be planned, even anticipated, but the day the penny drops and the bags are packed is one of the biggest hurdles in the process, in my opinion.

If you are leaving the family home, remember that you may not be allowed back in again until it is sold, if that is what is agreed. So make sure that you have packed accordingly. This means that you have your clothes, both work and casual, to allow you to go to work on the Monday and function normally, as if nothing has happened. If you are the breadwinner you are still going to need to do this and you will want to minimise the effects of the separation as much as possible.

Although you may well have a 'Right of Occupation' (to use a legal term) at your home if you are the 'jumper', the reality of achieving this may be possibly untenable. It can cause significant stress to all parties and you may want to consider carefully if you want to pursue this right.

If the house is to be sold, it will still need to be kept in good condition to ensure that you achieve a fair price so keep the situation amicable where possible.

d. Some money business

It is not long before the subject of money is going to enter this topic and I thought now would be a good juncture to introduce a few issues that you might want to consider.

The joint account

I have heard a tale or two where a spouse has informed their other half that they are leaving for this or that reason. They are obviously and rightly concerned that the spouse is not going to react well to this announcement, although many people in this position take a more mature approach to what may have been inevitable.

However, it is to an extent only natural that some people will revert to the instinct of protecting themselves from the financial consequences of the division, by taking what they can as soon as they can. People have stripped joint accounts, even overdrawn them on purpose, to make sure that they have cash with which to protect themselves.

So, before you think that your partner is going to sit there bewailing the loss of your undying love, think about the other side of the coin and prepare for your own shock.

Your spouse may be tougher than you think!

Yes, you do have to pay the bills . . . it's just sensible planning

You will have a credit rating even if you are not aware of it.

A 'credit rating' is a calculated score that applied to your financial records based on your ability to borrow and repay debt, such as credit cards, mortgages, loans and as suggested above, a tenancy agreement. A divorce in itself may negatively affect this rating and your overall creditworthiness.

So why should you be concerned about this?

This credit rating can be adversely affected by missed payments to loan agreements, such as mortgages or car finance. Although this may sound the least of your worries, you are still going to want to move on after a divorce and this may involve another mortgage or other credit agreements. A poor credit rating during divorce may affect your ability to get back on the property ladder later. So make sure that attention is paid to keeping the existing bills and monthly payments up to date and correct, even if you don't have use of the house or car during the divorce process.

Final affordability

This leads on to the affordability of where you and your spouse are going to live in the event of a separation and divorce. In recent economic times there have been many stories of couples remaining under the same roof because neither of them could afford to live somewhere else. With UK house prices having fallen and unlikely to recover for some time, this situation may continue. I salute those that can amicably achieve this compromise.

Again, this boils down to good financial planning and co-operation between both parties, to allow dignity and sanity to remain in place during the divorce process. It may take some time to resolve. You will both have to remain housed, warm, fed and in a position to be able to deal with the matters at hand.

Working together, where possible, for the good of each other's long term financial futures, even though not together, will be well worthwhile however awkward at the time.

Emergency deposit funds

There are some basic financial planning cornerstones that I would always consider prudent, irrespective of whether you are going through a divorce or not. The first one is to make a will, which I have commented on further in Section f, later.. Another financial planning suggestion is to try to maintain three to six months' readily available deposit funds in case of emergencies. This unforeseen problem might be the car breaking down or the freezer 'dying' or the roof leaking. It might also be just taking a quick holiday to get away from the drudgery of the 'rat race'.

From a tax planning point of view it is unusual to see both parties in a marriage sharing a similar income tax rate. Each individual has been taxed separately since around 1990, where couples were taxed on income together prior to this date. One partner may be at home caring for the family, possibly taking on part-time work, while the other may be a basic or higher rate taxpayer, keeping the household finances afloat. Therefore, it may be sensible to maintain any emergency savings in the name of the lower rate taxpayer. There is no point in giving the taxman extra income if it can be sensibly and legally avoided.

However, this in itself could create a dilemma. If a marriage breaks down and you are the one without the savings, how are you going to afford the deposit on a rental property if you decide that you are going to live separately? If the separation is a mutual decision, then one party may well be willing to hand over a proportion of their sole savings pot to help alleviate the stress of both parties being under the same roof. Then again, one partner may well be reluctant to hand over a cup of tea, let alone any cash. If you are a higher rate taxpayer, then as examples, you might want to think about holding some emergency cash in your own name using other savings options, such as tax efficient cash ISAs or even Premium Bonds. This may give you a greater level of liquidity at a time of need.

e. Some social effects

Telling the folk

Think carefully about who else you are going to tell, because other members of your family will need to know what is going on and will want to offer support where they can. Don't let them phone you at home one evening, only to be coolly informed that you have jumped ship or been dumped with the implication that you have also left the family destitute. Be proactive after the event to make sure that you control the situation.

The day you decide to leave, if in fact it is you who are doing the leaving, may not be fully anticipated and close family will want to know that you are safe.

The parting of the friends

Don't forget that all the assets of the marriage are usually divided — and this can include the friends and in some cases even relatives. Mention the 'D' word (divorce) and you can sometimes watch them scatter as though it were something contagious.

The dear 'friends' that you have known for years, first as, your own friends and then as a couple, may evaporate in the flurry of mudslinging that follows the parting pair. This might be because they have been poisoned against you before you can do any poisoning yourself, if you feel the urge.

Friends might find the situation threatening because it could identify weaknesses in their own union. Or it may be that the talk of divorce becomes boring after the fifth repetition of how your soon to be ex-spouse is manipulating you for everything (along with their solicitors) from anything from your pension to your current account. The friends might even be the cause of the problem with your marriage.

Whichever category they fit, the division of friends is something that can only be sadly endured.

Friends and acquaintances usually feel that they have three choices. The warring couple will usually want them to see one party or the other, but not both — although they have no right to stipulate this. You can hear it now: 'you can't be friends with them!'

Do they go with their *original* friend, the one they first knew? This is usually where the allegiance lies. Or do they continue to see the one they perceive as the aggrieved party? Or, finally, do they just take their leave from the whole situation to avoid the problem? Some friends will do that, as it seems like the path of least resistance. If they do, were they worth knowing in the first place?

Remember that you are still a good person. You will recover. You may re-marry or have another partner, and you will certainly still be part of the community. In my experience, the friends that walk away are the friends who later regret withdrawing their support. You will know which camp you are in when you bump into them in the street, as you have done for years, and the conversation and body language are rather awkward, stilted and most of all short!

You have been judged and sentenced. Be ready!

f. The time to accept that a divorce is on its way

If you have discussed and helped a partner understand this situation and did not find it difficult then you probably had a more understanding spouse than many. Maybe this is a sign that you should not have asked for the divorce in the first place.

This stage is not going to be easy. However, you have to go through it because on some grounds your partner will have to sign the divorce papers at some point in the future — unless you wait around for five years, which does happen occasionally. There are some legal exceptions to this point, but in most cases divorce papers will need to be signed.

The final nail in the coffin of a marriage may take some time for one party to accept. They will have to do it at their own pace and this has to be understood.

I have spoken to many divorcing people who are simply devastated that their spouse has left. It takes them many months, if not years to truly recover from this new reality. They may be unable to make any financial decisions for a significant period of time, until they can see what they want from their future life on their own — and how much it is all going to cost.

If divorce is what you want, then a spectrum of emotions may come out. And just like a rainbow, you never know where they are going to appear, how long they will last and that there is certainly no pot of gold at the end of it. Fear, anger, regret, remorse, resignation, understanding, acceptance may all be experienced by both parties at this time and during the overall process. I think that it is worthwhile understanding that these emotions may come in that order for you and that your spouse may be at a different stage in these waves of emotion next time you see them. You may want to be prepared and sympathetic to these phases as they occur.

Obviously the party who is being left is likely to want to know *why*, and probably *who with* and *for how long?* Then the accusations of deceit will probably follow, quickly chased by anger, reflection, misunderstanding and fear. You may be caught off-guard by your partner's simple positive acceptance and desire to get this situation resolved promptly and simply. This can certainly be the case if an unhappy calm has lain over the household for some time.

You will know where you are in this cycle, or you will have a fair idea. After all, you did marry your spouse and I am sure you must know one or two of their traits by now.

Remember that all this may have an effect the on family and the health of both you and your soon to be ex-spouse.

Blood pressure tablets

Divorce can be an all-consuming affair. You have to run your normal life, working as hard as you can to ensure that the salary keeps coming in to pay for food and clothing as well as the mortgage on the house that you may no longer be living in. You may also have to meet the rental/lodging costs of the accommodation that you now abide in and your solicitor will also need paying. So, no pressure then!

It is easy to forget to look after yourself physically, as well as mentally, and to dismiss those aches and pains as the stress of the situation. I believe that stress has a natural home with divorce. Every twist and turn of the evolving structured mess will cause stress for both parties. It is also difficult to keep the effects of that stress from your children, getting caught in the crossfire.

Protect them from it all as much as you can. They will only have a lifetime of their own stress to look forward to anyway. That's modern life.

Think about your body's need and keep fit and lay off the red or white 'happy juice' in the evening. It's too easy to get into the habit of drowning your sorrows in a glass or three. Also, when left alone in your new, usually smaller accommodation, it is all too easy to order a takeaway rather than cook a meal with nutritious food. Cooking for one, or for the newly-reduced nuclear family, has never been great fun.

And no, opening solicitors' letters does not count as exercise! Keep an eye on your diet and stay focused on looking after yourself and your immediate dependents first, and secondly everyone else. You only have yourself to get you out of this mess, and being fit for the job may speed up the process. It will also keep you fresh for the fight when and if it comes.

Death and Wills

Protection is usually available to a legal spouse in the event of the death of his or her husband or wife. Some protection is available to a partner in the event of death after two years together, as he or she can make a claim on the estate of their deceased partner. One of the mainstays of any financial planning if you are in a relationship with a loved one is to make a Will. A Will details how you want your assets and chattels to be distributed in the event of your death. These can provide protection for your spouse, family, and partner. Many people do not like to face this reality or cannot afford the services of a legal adviser to get a Will drawn up. If cost is an issue, then use a 'Will kit' from any good stationers. In my opinion a cheap will is better than no Will at all.

Where to live?

Irrespective of what the asset is, many people have to sell capital items to fund separation and divorce. If you are going to find accommodation then think about where this should be. You are still going to want to provide housing for the children or accommodate them for visits, and still get to work to ensure that you can afford to pay all the bills.

You may not want to move to somewhere close to your former home, so make sure that you choose your location carefully in between any wrangling that may be going on with your partner.

g. Stating the reason for divorce

As noted at the beginning of this chapter, when you divorce, a fact (or reason) for the cause of the breakdown has to be specified. A Petition is prepared and is presented to the court to confirm that the marriage has broken down irretrievably and you are specifying the 'facts' of the breakdown on the divorce papers. If someone is divorcing you, you become the Respondent and your soon to be ex-spouse is the Petitioner. The five grounds of divorce in England and Wales are as follows:

- **Adultery** (with or without a named party)
  The meaning is obvious but remember, this will
  have to be proved if not admitted.

- **Unreasonable Behaviour**
  The allegations of unreasonable behaviour do
  not have to be severe for the court to consider
  them. It is only you who has to find them
  unreasonable, although the judge has to believe
  that the reasons provided are not trivial. A few
  examples may be needed to evidence this claim.

- **Desertion**
  This means that your spouse deserted you
  without your consent for a continuous period of
  at least two years. This reason is seldom used
  these days.

- **Two-year separation**
  This is where you and your spouse have been
  living apart for at least two years immediately
  preceding the presentation of the divorce
  Petition. You will also both be agreeing to a
  divorce for this to work.

- **Five-year separation**
  Again, you and your spouse have been living
  apart, but this time for at least five years
  immediately preceding the presentation of the
  divorce Petition. The difference here is that the
  spouse doesn't have to consent to the divorce.

The grounds for divorce are merely the mechanism to
get the process started. They are not a factor for the court
to consider.

Being awkward about the fact that you had something to do with the failure of a marriage is usually a recipe for higher costs and greater torment. No one is perfect so my suggestion would be to go with the path of least resistance if you want a smoother and cheaper path out of the marriage.

h. Instructing solicitors and the first letters

You *instruct* a solicitor to act on your behalf — however, you must understand early in the process that solicitors will only *act on your instructions*. They will carry out your will within the legal framework and, therefore, you have to be happy with your instructions as these will mould the final outcome.

This means they will deliver your instructions rather than provide their own instructions. Obviously they will give advice where appropriate, but they will tend to work from what you tell them you wish them to do. Solicitors undertake significant training to qualify and to provide you with the advice you require, using case law as a guide where required.

Think long and hard about any guidance you are given. You can spend many expensive hours trying to build a case with some parameters, where if you had put forward instructions more quickly you might have saved a lot of time and money. Remember that your solicitor does not have to live with the final result and outcome, you do!

Research and find a good solicitor and instruct them early, on day one, even if the divorce process is setting out to remain amicable. The solicitor will only write to your ex-spouse when you are ready and have instructed them accordingly.

A solicitor cannot accept instructions from both parties as this would be a conflict of interest. Ask a trusted friend, Accountant, Resolution contact or your Financial Adviser who to use. Also you need to know what you are looking for in a solicitor. To be frank, if you know that your ex-partner is likely to chase you for every penny and contest every detail of any agreement, even if these points of issue are trivial, make sure that your solicitor choice reflects this. It might be worth your while speaking to a few contacts before deciding who to use. There are now various choices in the overall process to employ.

Many of the legal profession as a whole are proffering the option of a mediated service which many people are finding a highly valuable and a less contentious legal process.

There are several options to choose from before you proceed with a divorce:

- **Own resolution**: The DIY approach, where you both work through the details and agree who is doing what and who is keeping what

- **Mediation**: Both parties use a mediation service to work through the process, using a neutral third party. The mediator prepares a summary of consensus which goes to each parties solicitor to formalise

- **Collaborative process**: Although you will both use a solicitor, both parties and their legal advisers work together to come to an amicable solution, opting out of the court process until you file the final documents

- **Negotiation via a solicitor**: You both appoint solicitors and negotiate an agreement between all four of you — the spouses and the solicitors. This path is usually used for contested cases. If this does not work it may revert to the use of the court process. Your solicitor can detail this to you.

Usually, the overall expense increases the further you travel down the above list. Also, some people are incapable of negotiating and only understand confrontation, which reduces the number of options available to the last one detailed above.

When you contact a solicitor you can discuss these options and to look at some form of collaboration to try to make the process less stressful as well as cheaper. This is called the *collaborative process.* You may want to ask at the outset if the solicitor and his or her partnership are advocates of this resource and why?

The collaborative process

I would like to observe early in this text that the legal profession in England and Wales has made significant advances in the last few years, and this is spreading. Lawyers have in many cases become less confrontational about divorce proceedings, with many now actively practising *collaborative* processes. Where a marriage has irretrievably broken down, this process allows couples with the help of their solicitors and other advisers to negotiate the terms and finances of any divorce separation in an open and mature fashion. This has the potential to save both time and money for all concerned, although the process does not suit everyone. I applaud the energy that many legal advisers and the organisation, Resolution, have shown in championing this cause. Discuss this option with your legal adviser before proceeding as both parties will need to agree to the process.

Although the collaborative law option does not work out for everyone who tries it, this is a process that has run well in America for some time and has been introduced into the British Isles by an organisation called Resolution. For information, Resolution also run programmes for parents on caring for children after a separation or divorce has occurred and how this can be effectively organised to minimise the effects of parting for the children. Ask your solicitor whether he or she is a member and an advocate of Resolution and the collaborative process. There are many Resolution accredited professionals across the majority of the UK.

In my opinion it is always worth at the very least giving this approach a chance, although your legal adviser will show you what is involved in the process before you start. You can start down the collaborative route, and then later, if you find that it is not working for you, you can agree to move away from this option and head down the negotiated or contested route if you prefer. Again take legal advice on this issue throughout the process.

As already noted, there are some people for whom a fight is the only option they understand. You will know whether you or your partner is one of these. Remember, you pay to argue! Taking this a stage further, if your case is or becomes contentious your solicitor may recommend the use of a barrister to negotiate your final agreement.

The use of a specialist barrister is likely to see your costs increase and you may want to discuss this possibility and the varying costs at the outset.

You don't need to use a solicitor to achieve a divorce. To agree the money side of things, you may be able to do most of the negotiations yourself without referring to a legal counsel, although many would not recommend this. To make any agreement final, it will need to be submitted to the court for approval as long as it is fair. It is possible to DIY your divorce and I have seen this done. However, if it goes wrong then you may find that you have jumped off a bigger cliff than you needed to. Think long and hard about choosing this option because it could cost you more in the long run.

All of your financial assets will need to be disclosed, whichever route you plan to take. The control of this process should be between you, your partner and your respective legal advisers. To help, you may want to look at the Form E, Financial Statement form at the end of this book now to begin to understand what is needed and this will involve.

As suggested earlier, be ready for your solicitors request for upfront fees on account and remember that they will need to see some identification for their records. You should always keep these documents safe anyway, and especially before you drop the bombshell about wanting a divorce, in case you find yourself being excluded from your home with immediate effect.

Whatever you do, keep focused and controlled in your approach and you will survive if not thrive at the end, as you will see.

Notes/ Questions to ask?

Notes/ Questions to ask?

Notes/ Questions to ask?

3. The Legals and Financials

a. The Petition

Once you have decided how you are going to approach your case, you may *petition* a court yourself for divorce or you may do it via your solicitor. As an alternative, you may be the Respondent to the petition put to you.

In petitioning, you are confirming that the marriage has irretrievably broken down and you are required to provide a reason for this, using one of the five 'fact' options given above (Chapter 2, Section g). Court proceedings in family law are confidential. The "fact" of the divorce can be disclosed, such as the reason for the petition, but the details of any adultery or unreasonable behaviour, for example, cannot.

The petition also includes a section referred to as the 'prayer', requesting that the divorce be granted. (I know of many people who *pray* that the circumstances of the divorce had never come about in the first place, but this is not the same thing.)

At the time of presenting the petition, you are likely to have to pay your first costs to the court (unless you are using the Legal Aid system) so be ready for this expense. Further details and the conditions to receive Legal Aid are detailed by the Legal Services Commission. Their website is: www.legalservices.gov.uk

At the same time, if there are children, an additional form has to be presented as a 'Statement of Arrangements', which outlines the arrangements for the children. Sensibly, the law encourages couples to try to agree these arrangements before the form is required or submitted, although this is not always the position.

By presenting a petition you do not have to prove your claim, such as adultery or unreasonable behaviour by the other party, although if it is not accepted by your spouse you may have to prove it. Dependent on your circumstances in your case, you may decide to evidence your petition by collecting proof. There are many professional investigation firms (Private Investigators) that can help you with the preparation of evidence that may be required (at cost) , although this is outside the scope of this text.

Costs

It is easy to forget the legal costs that can occur. Solicitors are not charitable organisations and they are in business to charge fees and these should be detailed in their opening documents. You may also have to pay your fees to the court, although the court hearings themselves do not attract a charge.

Discussing your case and the process/action that should be taken is vital to ensure that you don't agree to something that you later regret — but remember that solicitors will usually charge on a time basis in segments of say six minutes or ten minutes. So, using this example, if you start a conversation you will be charged for at least six or ten minutes, even if the call is much shorter than that. Most solicitors will also have an hourly rate and you might want to confirm this at the outset.

Some firms require a fee to be paid up front to retain their services. If your solicitor does, it will focus your mind quickly.

Learn from this and don't indulge in small talk. Before you pick up the phone, know exactly what you want to talk about and go straight to the issue at hand, however much you may like your solicitor personally. To achieve this you may want to write your thoughts, questions and requirements out and, in fact, avoid the telephone and go straight to email with your bullet points. Escalating costs may even focus your mind on agreeing negotiations directly with your ex-spouse to minimise your solicitors time (and costs). There are usually no winners in divorce and you do not want to make the legal profession the main benefactor from yours.

Set yourself a realistic financial floor when negotiating, below which you will not allow yourself to fall, or you may walk away with a poor settlement. However, this has to be balanced with the knowledge that *any* settlement you end up with may feel poor to you anyway. Your solicitor will guide you.

From a financial planning point of view, try to 'pay as you go' with your legal costs. Your solicitor will prefer this. It also means that, when you hit the floor of your divorce jump, what's left is yours, rather than having to settle up with your legal team or pay interest on the sum you still owe them. Your solicitor will send you a Terms of Business at the outset of your agreement and instruction. Read through this before starting your negotiations to know how the cost side of things is going to work.

One recent initiative is for a solicitor to issue *divorce vouchers* to help with costs. These vouchers can be purchased by anyone and given to others as a gift to help with costs. It may not sound the most fun gift idea in the world, but the gesture is very welcome at what can be a time of financial hardship.

This issue can be extended to another financial issue: *cash flow*, which is the movement of money in and out of your finances or bank account.

You may have decided to move out of the matrimonial home and rent other accommodation elsewhere. This does not absolve you from paying the existing mortgage or council tax. Just because you are going through the transition of divorce does not mean that they will let you off the bill. So, as you would in any good business, take a look at your budget early in the process. Cash is king in business, and this likely to be the case for you personally too.

Becoming a divorce bore

As already noted, divorce can be an all-consuming affair at the best of times. This can have various effects and outcomes. Other people, such as legal advisers, will be regularly delving into your past life and deciding what you will have left at the end of the process.

It is good to talk to someone you trust. Make sure that you do speak to an independent third party who will provide some wise words when the chips are down. You know who the best person for this is, that constant one in your life who has always been there, possibly even since before your marriage. I would recommend that you avoid choosing the third party who may be the cause of the divorce as your confidant.

In my case, my father, Roger, kept me on the straight and narrow even though he knew little about divorce or its winding path. However, I have to admit that the second time around we were both revisiting old ground rather than breaking new turf. I will always be grateful to him for his time, especially when I would bore him rigid with the same issue yet again in an only slightly different format. You will probably believe that this different format is a radical departure from your previous statements and ideas; in reality, it will be the same old ground with most details unchanged.

By the way, once you have got these issues off your chest, don't go around repeating the same conversation with other people. After a while even your best friends will find you a *divorce bore*. I know this from experience. If you do not have access to a *wise old owl*, then try counselling. Contact Relate who will help you understand where you are emotionally in the overall divorce process.

There are many divorce coaches and counsellors who can help you through the process. Some people, mainly men, may regard this as a non-option — however, in return for a few hours of time and some financial commitment, it could prove highly valuable. Any information you provide is treated sympathetically and confidentially and you will only benefit if you're prepared to invest in it.

Wherever you decide to confide, be careful whom you choose. You would not wish your innermost thoughts or current circumstances to be inadvertently fed back to your ex-spouse, even by accident. If this happens, you may end up closing off *all* communication (usually permanently) to ensure that any 'leaks' cannot even begin to happen.

Becoming a divorce bragger

There is a flip side to every scenario and I am sure you'll agree that there is nothing so brash as a 'divorce bragger'.

Imagine you have been invited to a friend's party. You have been looking forward to this for weeks because these parties are usually quite lively, with new faces that you can investigate during the course of a late night out. Now imagine that you end up with the choice of standing in a corner with the divorce bore or, in the other corner, the divorce bragger. Nightmare!

We have seen how the divorce bore will handle things. Many people would argue that the divorce bragger is even worse. He or she is easily recognised by the 'how much I lost' conversation, 'of course I am still the primary carer' claim, or the ' . . . and I still managed to keep the house and move the girl/boyfriend in' boasts (this list may be endless!) that will be bandied about with the shallow sense of victory that few of us would wish to be part of.

Some shops have begun offering divorce lists, in the style of wedding lists, to allow friends and family to buy presents to *celebrate* a divorce and possibly replace the household goods and luxuries lost in the division of assets. A step too far for marketing? Time will tell.

b. Caring for and spending time with your children

During the course of writing this book, I have deliberately limited my comment on the issue of children. This is deliberate because this is truly a *specialist area* and one where I am not qualified to provide any guidance. There are many excellent counsellors who can work with both children and parents and I would recommend that you speak to them to get advice, if you need it. This will help in the process of separation/divorce to make proceedings more 'child centred' and ensure that any short or longer term psychological effects are kept to a minimum.

Children's needs are all different and I recommend parents contact the Family Mediation Council. Their up to date details can be found at www.familymediationcouncil. org.uk or you may want to speak to your GP for guidance on whom to talk to. You may also want to consider using Relate and further details are available on their website, www.relate.org.uk.

You should consult your ex-spouse on this point, as this may well be a joint responsibility. Whatever you do, if help is needed, seek advice promptly.

Children are our greatest asset and should be treated as such. They cannot be divided, only loved. They will need to understand what is going on so that they can adjust to the changed balance of their routine. They will have to master a new process in their lives to sort out how they are going to continue to see Mum or Dad.

The parents may no longer love each other, but the bond between parent and child cannot normally be fully broken. Your child will still love you if you are the 'jumper' from the family unit, however they may not understand and they may not agree with your decision. Just because you choose not to be with your partner any more does not mean that your child should be expected to stop loving your soon to be ex-spouse.

Your children's thoughts on why and how this division has occurred should be respected, even if you or the child cannot agree about the outcome. Your child may be angry or scared (or both) and you must be prepared for these reactions.

It is my belief that the commitment that you made to the marriage was no more serious than the commitment you made to the children of the marriage — and divorcing one's children is not an option. Although it may be difficult sometimes, be sure only ever to speak well of your ex-partner as you will always share the obligation of parenting to your child/children.

Creating a bolt-hole for you and the children

The greater the feeling of normality you can create for your children within your new lifestyle, the better. You can make a good start by gaining a bolt-hole that feels safe, comfortable and warm for both you and any visiting children. They may quickly start to feel more secure in knowing where you live, where their room is, where they put their clothes and how your TV works, as examples. Children need familiarity and the space to move around your new place, to know that they are welcome and still very much part of the family.

Both parties will have to agree to accommodate time and access and make it as friendly as possible in front of the children. They do not want to see you fighting, and you want to start your weekends with your children on a high note, not a negative one. You may not be delighted to see your ex-spouse, but I hope you will be pleased to see the children, even if that means you end up being the weekend chauffeur to their various social events.

This can be tricky if you separate to different geographical areas (and some divorcing partners have even been known to emigrate) so bear this in mind when you are finding alternative accommodation.

From a financial point of view, the children will need to be protected to ensure that their requirements and needs are met. In a financial settlement you will negotiate on the issue of whether you are paying maintenance for the care of one or more parties.

If you have any doubts about any aspect of this issue, seek advice from a specialist.

c. Maintenance

There are two types of maintenance: maintenance to the ex-spouse and child maintenance. I remember in the 1970s occasionally hearing the word *Alimony* and not knowing what it meant. If you pay maintenance you will know exactly what it is.

The agreed maintenance payments you make or receive will depend on what you negotiate. There may be no maintenance at all to be paid. However, if children are involved, this is unlikely.

You can negotiate for a 'clean break' from your ex-spouse, which means that no maintenance is paid to him or her. You cannot have a clean break from child maintenance. So, you could in principle have a clean break deal with your ex-spouse, but still be required to pay him or her child maintenance as an example. You could arrange to pay a regular instalment (usually monthly) broken down for each child until he or she reaches the age of majority or the end of education (possibly even university), and then pay separate maintenance for the ex-spouse.

The payment of maintenance can be increased with inflation each year if required and can be renegotiated up or down at a later date during its tenure should financial situations change. Due to the recent economic climate, many maintenance agreements have been revisited and revised accordingly.

Child Support Agency (CSA)

In some cases it is possible to involve other organisations, such as the Child Support Agency (CSA), which is part of the Child Maintenance and Enforcement Commission. The CSA's role is to make sure that parents who live apart from their children contribute financially to their upkeep by paying child maintenance. You may want to look at their main website, which is www.csa.gov.uk.

Many will know that the CSA was first introduced in 1994 and has been controversial ever since in its application of collecting maintenance payments. The website is useful in updating your understanding of their current role and the parameters to which it works. The agency's role is ever evolving and changing and it might pay you to keep yourself updated.

The CSA uses information provided by both parties in the divorce, to understand and consider whether someone has to pay child maintenance, if used. The agency also works out the amount of maintenance that should be paid. It may also use information from other sources, including the non-resident parent's employer or HM Revenue & Customs (HMRC) — the department that used to be known as the Inland Revenue, to check income levels.

The CSA calculates child maintenance by applying one of four rates to the non-resident parent's income. For information, *Income* includes earnings, tax credits and money from pensions. As an example, the CSA uses the amount of income left after such outgoings as income tax, National Insurance and any money paid into a pension scheme have been deducted, although there are some exceptions.

To take this a stage further, the four current rates (2009/2010) that can be applied to the non-resident parent's income are:

- **Basic rate**: income of £200 or more per week

- **Reduced rate**: income of more than £100 and less than £200 per week

- **Flat rate**: income of between £5 and £100 per week

- **Nil rate**: income of less than £5 per week

The Child Support Agency can then adjust the child maintenance based on varying factors, such as:

- The number of children for whom the non-resident parent needs to pay child maintenance

- Whether the child stays with the non-resident parent at least one night each week

- The number of other children who are living with the non-resident parent, for whom they or their partner claim Child Benefit (this being a regular payment made to anyone bringing up children)

Child Maintenance Calculator

The CSA website has a page that allows you to feed in your circumstances and income details to arrive at an indicative figure of the likely maintenance that they would expect you to pay, based on their understandings.

The calculation and outcome of this system may vary from that used by your solicitor and you may wish to discuss this with them accordingly.

For how long do you have to pay maintenance to your ex-spouse?

You can negotiate within the financial settlement an agreement that the receiving spouse will only receive the payments provided he or she does not cohabit with anyone else for a period of time. Maintenance from a former spouse terminates on re-marriage.

An alternative to this is that the maintenance payment is time-limited, for example, to a retirement age or a fixed date in the future, such as five or ten years hence. A time limit is usual, although there are some life-orders for long marriages.

Another option, if you want to avoid contact with the ex-spouse, is to capitalise all of the maintenance payments and then pay this as a lump sum, usually paid up front soon (if not immediately) after settlement. This may provide security to the receiving spouse and remove any ambiguity as to whether a payment is going to be made. I have seen this occurring more often in older couples divorcing, allowing them an effective clean break in retirement. It may offer both parties the freedom to cohabit or remarry soon after the divorce and financial settlement are agreed and paid.

Therefore, you can see that the negotiation that is made can provide the opportunity for many variant outcomes. You may pay or receive a capital sum for the upkeep and lifestyle of the soon to be ex-spouse and the children. If a regular maintenance payment is agreed, this can also be to the ex-spouse or for the children or both. This is where good legal advice is vital.

While both parties are inching towards this negotiated settlement you will need to be paying or receiving funds in the meantime to keep the family ship afloat whilst both parties agree terms. You should pay or receive immediate maintenance — but think carefully about what *levels* are to be paid. It may take months to reach a settlement and the interim maintenance level could set a precedent for what should be paid in the future. Being generous at this point may prove costly in the longer run. Take legal advice from your solicitor on this topic as early as possible.

The children do not need spoiling just because their parents are divorcing. However, they do need the same level of attention from both parties, although this will now be staggered over different time slots, rather than taking place at the same time within the same household. As already noted, many specialist organisations can help specifically with counselling for children, to help them with their own journey through their parents' divorce. Where appropriate, keep your children updated on progress in a fair and positive fashion.

Divorce for any couple with children is a difficult time and these pressures are likely to continue long after the divorce is settled and everyone continues with their lives.

A recent BBC documentary, *Who Needs Fathers? The Right to be a Dad* (2010) detailed statistics that showed that fathers who lose contact with their children (nearly 40%) usually do so within two years of separation. You may currently believe that all is amicable with your separation, and that the new dissected family will survive the trauma of divorce — but think carefully about what could happen and be prepared.

Ex-spouses do move on and find new employment and people to love. The world does not stop turning or changing. In the United States, the divorce system in many states has introduced 'parenting after parting' courses championed by the Resolution organisation to help children stay in contact with their parents. I understand that in some American states, it is *mandatory* for parents to attend a course before a court will grant a divorce. The English and Welsh legal profession has shown interest in this process and I applaud this initiative.

d. Opening financial negotiations: who's keeping what?

Inevitably the subjects of the various money and assets of the marriage are going to raise their heads during your negotiations. Thinking about the money side of things, you should start by listing the assets that you jointly hold. This may include the house and savings, but then needs to move on to the less obvious assets such as pensions. Pension values are added into the equation — and if you have a final salary scheme, this can have a high monetary value.

Before you get too embroiled in the divorce process, even if it is amicable, you may want to make a note of the financial assets as you understand them. Think about it in these terms:

- What assets you hold?

- What assets you think your ex-spouse holds?

- What assets you jointly own?

This may provide you with a ready-reckoner later in negotiations, just in case suggestions come forward that may have forgotten that old (but surprisingly valuable) endowment policy or pension from the company you were working for when you first met. For information, lost pensions can be found using a tracing service from the Department for Social Development. Their website is www.dsdni.gov.uk.

e. Agreeing the structure of the financial separation

At the outset you are likely to have a fair idea of what assets you and your spouse own in terms of cash, assets, property and pensions as examples. You may also know approximately what income was coming into the household. Bank Statements are a good source of information. There will be variances to the overall inputs, with, as an example, one party to the marriage having a far greater capacity to earn than the other and this may well be taken into account when dividing up capital because of their ability to take on mortgage finance and find (and pay for) alternative accommodation.

In the financial agreement you may well be looking at separating two things: Income and capital/pensions.

As suggested earlier, you may want to start listing out assets at an early stage whilst your memory is clear. One way to focus the mind on what you can expect to discuss in your divorce is to look at the Form E financial form in the appendix at the rear of this book. I have considered this further in the next section.

The Financial Statement, Form E

Not everyone needs to complete a Form E, but you should take advice on this from your legal adviser. Whether or not you use this form, a full financial disclosure in some format will be required for a financial settlement.

You will need at some point to agree the financial settlement between both parties. To do this, you need to know what you have financially, in terms of income, pensions, debts and assets. In the collaborative process you may gather this information together (possibly using a Form E) and share the findings to allow an agreement to be reached without contention. For contested divorces (and for some others) a Form E may well be used.

I have attached a copy of a Form E to Appendix 1 because it is a long and detailed document encompassing all aspects of your financial history to date. It can be quite daunting when you first see it and you will note that if you are submitting one it will need to be sworn to confirm that the information provided is complete and accurate.

The form acts as a Financial Fact Find, giving all your financial details, including income and assets and details of your needs. It's actually quite a good cash flow tool in thinking about your incomings and outgoings to assess your overall financial needs. Usually, both you and your spouse will complete separate Form Es and they can be submitted to the court as a declaration of personal wealth, with any attaching evidence/documents required. They are legally binding, so make sure that you complete yours accurately.

Usually if a Form E is required, then both parties may exchange Form Es to see who has what in order to start the process of negotiation. You might want to check this point with your solicitor before you hand over your full details to make sure that a similar document is coming back.

Most solicitors will look for a reasonable split of assets and income, taking into account that any children will need to be protected and housed appropriately. The question has to be what the definition of *'reasonable'* is! Any children of the marriage are the priority of the court (as well as the parents I hope) and their protection is paramount.

To be specific, the main factors laid down by Parliament, which the court will take into account when dealing with the financial aspects of a divorce are:

1. All the circumstances of the case put before it. Each marriage is different so every case is unique

2. The welfare of any minor children of the family under age 18. The court must give first consideration to this

These first two are clear enough. However, the court will consider some additional factors listed below. This list is not exhaustive and I would recommend that you speak to your solicitor to clarify these further.

3. Additional matters: ages, standard of living, needs and obligations/responsibilities, contributions made, income and earning capacity, lost value (for example in pensions), conduct, length of marriage

There is no simple answer to these matters because we are all different. All I can offer here are some additions that may provide you with some focus.

Housing

If the house equity and assets outside any pension value are high, then a split is usually sought by 'offsetting' their values. So, if the spouse who is looking after children needs to be housed, you might mutually decide that the main home is sold. One party might get the equity to re-home the family whilst the other keeps his or her pension and some cash to allow for a deposit to buy a separate home (possibly suitable for visiting or housing children) with a mortgage financed from income.

As we have seen in recent economic times, the equity in property values has tended to wane, which has caused some problems for offsetting. It has been known for one spouse to keep on the original mortgage as this is the only way of housing the family, whilst they then move and live elsewhere. This may mean that they would be entitled to an equity split in the home, but only when the property is sold — and that may only be when the children reach a certain age, such as majority at 18. The time parameters of this arrangement are usually agreed by both parties in the final financial settlement.

Pensions

This can be a complicated subject and you should seek advice on the approach used.

It may be possible in your case that a pension share may be involved. This may involve both parties getting some property equity, but this equity is effectively traded for a part share of a pension value. If agreement is reached, then a pension share order (or *Pension Annex*) will be granted by the court and the percentage of the pension that is to be split away is usually transferred out to another pension arrangement of the recipient's choice, dependent on the scheme. Also note that any agreed transfer out of a pension may incur administration fees by the original provider concerned and I have considered the issue of pensions and their benefits in detail further in Chapter 5.

There was another alternative for pension benefit division introduced in 1995 Pensions Act called *Earmarking*. This has not been widely used because it may not achieve a 'clean break' in pension terms and does not allow the ex-spouse to receive a pension income until the originating spouse with the pension fund actually draws benefits and retires. Death and remarriage will also effect this option. Some pension providers, usually final salary schemes, allow the share to stay within the scheme, although this is not always the case. If this is achievable then it should be considered carefully along with any other options. You should speak to a qualified Independent Financial Adviser (IFA) about the options available, but I recommend that you search hard for an adviser who knows the subject well as it is a specialist area.

Whatever you do, get independent financial advice on the real monetary values of what you and your partner hold in pensions, as an example. This is partly because you do not want to give away too much, and also because the true income value of a pension, for example, is not reduced or lost by transferring a cash equivalent transfer value (CETV) to an ex-spouse. For further information on CETV see chapter 5.

The independent financial adviser can be instructed by you individually or, with agreement, both parties to get an overall view of the financial situation to demonstrate true values of pensions and there benefits. Some IFAs are affiliated and accredited by the organisation Resolution and it might be worth your while enquiring about this accreditation from your financial adviser as their numbers have been growing across the UK. They have received training and testing as a 'Financial Neutral' in helping a separating couple with the pensions and financial affairs in divorce situations.

Financial Impasse

Many couples have decided to defer divorce proceedings because of the current economic climate. They simply cannot afford to sell the house or are not able to arrange suitable mortgage finance for the 'buyout' of the other spouse. This creates an awkward situation to say the least. You should still see a solicitor and an independent financial adviser if this happens to you to see if help can be applied to creating an alternative option.

If financial information is not forthcoming from a spouse in the process of divorce, it is possible to apply to the court to gain access to financial information, such as bank statements. Be aware though that this can be costly, in terms of both time and money.

Remember your solicitor's key role . . .

Getting financial advice from a qualified financial adviser (both independent and Resolution accredited) on your finances at an early stage is vital.

However, please note that it was never the role of your financial adviser to tell you how to divide assets. This is one of the most important aspects of your solicitor's role with their professional understanding of family law and its requirements and rules — either in the form of collaboration or by negotiation with the other party's solicitor. He or she will use case law and experience to work on your behalf and with your help, to ensure that you receive a reasonable division. Your case may set a precedent, but most cases use the precedent of other cases.

Notes/ Questions to ask?

4. From Decree Nisi to Decree Absolute and all documentation in between

Getting a *Decree Nisi* is quite straightforward when proceedings are not contested. Some people argue that this is why there has been a proliferation of 'DIY' divorces in the past few years. The *Decree Nisi* Dissolution Form is what really starts the dissolution of the marriage and says that you are on your way to freedom, if that is what you want.

A definition of a *Decree Nisi* is: *a decree nisi (non-absolute ruling) is a ruling by a court that does not have any force until such time that a particular condition is met. Once the condition is met the ruling becomes decree absolute and is binding (source: Wikipedia).*

Your case will be allocated a case number, which I am sure will become so familiar that you can quote it without thinking. When the court gives the Petitioner the *Decree Nisi*, the Petitioner has to wait six weeks and one day before he or she can make the divorce final by applying to the court for a *Decree Absolute*. Only the *Petitioner* (or their solicitor) can apply for the *Decree Absolute* in this timescale. However, the *Respondent* can apply after an additional three months (after the original six weeks and one day) but this may involve a court hearing. This is to allow time for anyone who objects to the divorce to tell the court why they object. You could almost call it a cooling off period, although if it has got this far it is unlikely that any cooling off will happen.

You are unlikely to apply for your *Decree Absolute* until you have an agreed and fully documented financial settlement in place, signed, sealed and delivered. The *Decree Absolute* means your divorce is completed and you are no longer married to your spouse.

However, invariably the problems start when you get to the division of assets and money. Who is going to get what, and who is going to trade the value of X asset, say the pension, for the value of Y asset, say the equity in the house. Whichever way the assets are carved up, the outcome is not going to look pretty from either party's point of view. Many DIY approaches to divorce come unstuck at this financial point.

From a personal point of view the *Decree Nisi* seems to mean very little. It is a single court-stamped piece of paper stating a date, both parties' full names and that a *Decree Nisi* Dissolution document has been granted by the court to which the Petitioner applied. In a way, this puts a flag in the sand to say you are on the way, but in reality it is only at Base Camp One on the journey of divorce to conquer the mountain of other hurdles. Obviously, this document is usually accompanied with a matching letter with an invoice in it. However, usually you will need a *Decree Nisi* to be able to submit your financial settlement for approval.

An example *Decree Nisi* Dissolution document can be seen below.

Decree Nisi - Dissolution (General Form)
MATRIMONIAL CAUSES ACT 1983
Family Proceedings Rules (Rule 2.43)

In the		
		County Court
Case No.		
Petitioner		
Respondent		
Co-Respondent		

Before [District] [His] [Her] [Honour] Judge

Sitting at

on the   day of   19   .

The Court held that

the respondent has

that the marriage solemnised

on the   day of   19   .

at

between

and

the Petitioner

the Respondent

has broken down irretrievably and decreed that the said marriage be dissolved unless sufficient cause be shown to the Court **within six weeks** from the making of this decree why such decree should not be made absolute.

Notes

This is not the final decree. Application for the final decree (decree absolute) must be made to the court. (For guidance see leaflet D187 'I have a decree nisi - what must I do next?')

Appeals: showing cause why this decree nisi should not be made final (absolute) is **not** an appeal against the decree nisi.

- If the decree nisi was pronounced by a district judge and the respondent wishes to appeal, he or she must serve notice of appeal and set **down the appeal** at this court **within 14 days** of the date of the decree nisi.

- If the decree nisi was pronounced by a judge and the respondent wishes to appeal, he or she must serve notice of appeal and set down the appeal in the Court of Appeal **within 4 weeks** of the date of the decree nisi.

The court office at

is open between 10 am and 4 pm Monday to Friday. Address all communications to the Court Manager and quote the case number.

D29 Decree Nisi - Dissolution (general form) - Matrimonial Causes Act 1983 - Family Proceedings Rules (rule 2.43)

© **Crown copyright**

Financial settlement

As part of your ongoing negotiations, you will have been discussing and agreeing how the assets of the marriage, such as the capital, income and liabilities are to be divided. This will be agreed with each spouse and each solicitor, in conjunction with any respective barristers that may have been used. This financial settlement is likely to be drawn up from the information provided in your now sworn Form E or alternative financial disclosure if this format was used. You can see the importance of providing full information at the outset because it will be this that is likely to be used in the finalised document presented to court.

Once negotiated, the agreed terms will be specifically documented in a Consent Order and signed by both spouses and their respective solicitors. This will form the template, almost an individual instruction manual of how to proceed financially after the *Decree Absolute* (your divorce) is granted. Remember you have signed to agree to these terms and that these will have been accepted by the court. This document will then again be stamped by the court, thereby finalising the financial agreement.

I have not been able to provide an example of this document because each is highly specific to each marriage and the assets of that marriage.

Decree Absolute

The postman delivers the day's collection of bills and junk mail offers, among which you open an envelope from your solicitors to say that you have a court-stamped *Decree Absolute*, illustrated on the next page, and an agreed financial settlement (Consent Order). You may have also received a Pension Sharing Order (s) or *Annex*, which will now need to be implemented.

I explain further how the pension situation can work in the next chapter, but have added an example of the pension *Annex* document below for reference to the *Decree Absolute,* if required.

Congratulations — or commiserations, whichever you prefer — you are now divorced. For many people, this is the first and possibly the only official physical evidence that the divorce is happening, along with the financial settlement . . . and usually an invoice.

This can be a distressing time for many.

An example *Decree Absolute* document can be seen below:

In the   County Court

No. of Matter

Between _____ Petitioner

and _____ Respondent

and _____ Co-respondent

Referring to the decree made in this cause on the

   day of   whereby it was decreed that

the marriage solemnised on the   day of

at

between

             the Petitioner

and

             the Respondent

be dissolved unless sufficient cause be shown to the Court within [six]

weeks from the making thereof why the said decree should not be made absolute, and no such cause having

been shown, it is hereby certified that the said decree was on the   day of

made final and absolute and that the said marriage was thereby dissolved.

Dated

Notes:

1. Divorce affects inheritance under a will

  Where a will has already been made by either party to a marriage then, by virtue of section 18A of
  the Wills Act 1837:

  (a) any provisions of the will appointing the former spouse executor or trustee or conferring a power of
    appointment on the former spouse shall take effect as if the former spouse had died on the date on
    which the marriage is dissolved unless a contrary intention appears in the will;

  (b) any property which, or an interest in which, is devised or bequeathed to the former spouse shall
    pass as if the former spouse had died on the date on which the marriage is dissolved unless a
    contrary intention appears in the will.

2. Divorce affects the appointment of a guardian

  Unless a contrary intention is shown in the instrument of appointment, any appointment under section 5(3) or
  (4) of the Children Act 1989 by one spouse of his or her former spouse as guardian is, by virtue of section 6
  of that Act, deemed to have been revoked at the date of dissolution of the marriage.

Address all communications to the Chief Clerk and quote the above case number.

The Court Office at

is open from 10 am to 4 pm Mondays to Fridays only

Certificate making Decree Nisi Absolute (Divorce)
Family Proceedings Rule 2.51 (2) (Form M9)
D37

An example *Pension Sharing Annex* document can be seen below:

Pension Sharing Annex under [section 24B of the Matrimonial Causes Act 1973] [paragraph 15 of Schedule 5 to the Civil Partnership Act 2004]	In the
	*[County Court] *[Principal Registry of the Family Division]

Case No. *Always quote this*	
Transferor's Solicitor's reference	
Transferee's Solicitor's reference	

Between   **(Petitioner)**

and   **(Respondent)**

Take Notice that:

On _____ the court

- made a pension sharing order under Part IV of the Welfare Reform and Pensions Act 1999.
- [varied] [discharged] an order which included provision for pension sharing under Part IV of the Welfare Reform and Pensions Act 1999 and dated _____ .

This annex to the order provides the person responsible for the pension arrangement with the information required by virtue of rules of court:

_____

A. Transferor's Details

(i)   The full name by which the Transferor is known:

(ii)   All names by which the Transferor has been known:

(iii) The Transferor's date of birth:

(iv) The Transferor's address:

(v)   The Transferor's National Insurance Number:

B. Transferee's Details

(i)   The full name by which the Transferee is known:

(ii)   All names by which the Transferee has been known:

(iii) The Transferee's date of birth:

(iv) The Transferee's address:

(v)   The Transferee's National Insurance Number:

(vi) If the Transferee is also a member of the pension scheme from which the credit is derived, or a beneficiary of the same scheme because of survivor's benefits, the membership number:

_____ Page 1 _____

Form P1 Pension Sharing Annex under section 24B of the Matrimonial Causes Act 1973 or under paragraph 15 of Schedule 5 to the Civil Partnership Act 2004   (12.05)   HMCS

C. **Details of the Transferor's Pension Arrangement**

(i) Name of the arrangement:

(ii) Name and address of the person responsible for the pension arrangement:

(iii) Policy Reference Number:

(iv) If appropriate, such other details to enable the pension arrangement to be identified:

(v) The specified percentage of the member's CETV to be transferred:

_____.____%

D. **Pension Sharing Charges**

It is directed that:

* The pension sharing charges be apportioned between the parties as follows:

or

* The pension sharing charges be paid in full by the Transferor.

(*Delete as appropriate)

E.

Have you filed Form M1 (Statement of Information for a Consent Order)?

If 'Yes' delete the text opposite.

Yes ☐   No ☐

The parties certify that:

(i) they have received the information required by Regulation 4 of the Pensions on Divorce etc (Provisions of Information) Regulations 2000;

(ii) that information is attached on Form P (Pension Inquiry Form); and

(iii) it appears from that information that there is power to make an order including provision under [section 24B of the Matrimonial Causes Act 1973] [paragraph 15 of Schedule 5 to the Civil Partnership Act 2004].

F.

In cases where the Transferee has a choice of an internal or external transfer, if the Transferee has indicated a preference, indicate what this is.

Internal Transfer ☐   External Transfer ☐

G. **In the case of external transfer only (recommended but optional information)**

(i) The name of the qualifying arrangement which has agreed to accept the pension credit:

(ii) The address of the qualifying arrangement:

(iii) If known, the Transferee's membership or policy number in the qualifying arrangement and reference number of the new provider:

Form P1   Page 2

G. Continued

(iv) The name, or title, business address, phone and fax numbers and email address of the person who may be contacted in respect of the discharge of liability for the pension credit on behalf of the Transferee:

(This may be an Independent Financial Advisor, for example, if one is advising the Transferee or the new pension scheme itself)

(v) Please attach a copy of the letter from the qualifying arrangement indicating its willingness to accept the pension credit.

Please complete boxes H to J where applicable

H.

Where the credit is derived from an occupational scheme which is being wound up, has the Transferee indicated whether he wishes to transfer his pension credit rights to a qualifying arrangement?　　Yes ☐　　No ☐

I.

Where the pension arrangement has requested details of the Transferee's health, has that information been provided?　　Yes ☐　　No ☐

J.

Where the pension arrangement has requested further information, has that information been provided?　　Yes ☐　　No ☐

Note: Until the information requested in A, B, (and as far as applicable G, H, I and J) is provided the pension sharing order cannot be implemented although it may be made. Even if all the information requested has been provided, further information may be required before implementation can begin. If so, reasons why implementation cannot begin should be sent by the pension arrangement to the Transferor and Transferee within 21 days of receipt of the pension sharing order and this annex.

THIS ORDER TAKES EFFECT FROM the date on which the Decree Absolute of Divorce or Nullity of marriage is granted, or the Final Order of Dissolution or Nullity of civil partnership is made, or if later, either

　　a. 21 days from the date of this order, unless an Appeal has been lodged, in which case
　　b. the effective date of the order determining that appeal.

To the person responsible for the pension arrangement:
　　*(*Delete as appropriate)*

*1. Take notice that you must discharge your liability within, the period of 4 months beginning with the later of:
　　• the day on which this order takes effect; or
　　• the first day on which you are in receipt of –
　　a. the pension sharing order including this annex (and where appropriate any attachments);
　　b. in a matrimonial cause, a copy of the decree of divorce or nullity of marriage and a copy of the certificate that the decree has been made absolute;
　　c. in a civil partnership cause, a copy of the final order of dissolution or order of nullity of civil partnership and a copy of the certificate that the order has been made final;
　　d. the information specified in paragraphs A, B and C of this annex and, where applicable, paragraphs G to J of this annex; and
　　e. payment of all outstanding charges requested by the pension scheme.

*2. The court directs that the implementation period for discharging your liability should be determined by regulations made under section 34(4) or 41(2)(a) of the Welfare Reform and Pensions Act 1999, in that:

Page 3

Form P1

Notes/ Questions to ask?

5. All the paperwork is done, now what?

Once you have received your various court stamped documents, you may be overjoyed at your release or, like many people, you may be hit hard by the realisation that you now have to start all over again. Please remember that the court papers are the detail of what has been agreed and confirm the way forward. This is only the beginning of getting what has been agreed settled.

For some, this may be a strange and melancholy day. On one hand there is the relief of knowing that everything has been agreed and approved by the court. Great! At last you know what the settlement looks like, although you are not out of the woods yet because everyone has to implement what was agreed. It may have taken you a long time to get these various documents and they are all very uninspiring once they arrive. Do remember to keep them safe because you will need them in the future, especially if you decide to marry again.

On the other hand, it does mean that a chapter of your life is closed and another one opened. Many of the good memories that you once enjoyed may have been eroded by the process of the divorce, however a new beginning beckons even if this seems rather daunting at first.

At least a framework has been created for you to detail how a division of assets is to be arranged, although this in itself may not stop the niggles at this late stage in the process.

Using this framework, you may now need to deal with what has been agreed. Some potential examples are listed below, although this is not an exhaustive list.

Sell the house

This may not be required as part of the settlement, but it may be more of an emotional issue of starting again in a new environment. You may come to feel that by selling up you are undertaking a cleansing process to ensure that the desired fresh start really is a *fresh start*.

At the time of any economic recovery, you may see the divorce rate recover because the window of opportunity to separate financially is available once more because of increasing property values, for example.

However, it is likely that selling your house may be part of the settlement agreed because it is understandably one of the biggest matrimonial assets and this will need to be undertaken quickly. Working together on this to achieve the best price is well worthwhile to help each party into the future.

Remember that there are likely to be legal, estate agent and removal costs in selling and you should check these at an early stage to ensure you know what these are for your future budgeting.

Re-mortgage

One alternative to the sale of the matrimonial home is that one partner effectively 'buys out' the other by financing the equity share through new mortgage finance to buy out the former spouse.

This may only be achievable by securing new mortgage finance and in the current economic climate this may prove difficult. Most mortgage lenders take into account your earnings ability (after the deduction of any income liabilities, such as a new maintenance agreement) and the remaining equity in the home before making a decision on how and whether they can help. If this is the option you plan to use, ensure that you start the approval process early because you may need to tie in the mortgage completion with the financial settlement — and as you have already seen, this may take time.

Also bear in mind that there are again usually legal and survey costs to achieve a re-mortgage and your mortgage adviser should be able to confirm the level of these before you proceed.

Relocation

This is also the time that access to children may become difficult because an ex-spouse moves on in terms of both love life and geographical location.

Even though an agreed contact programme is in place, the reality of a move to another part of the UK is still possible, depending on their needs and desires. Your ex-spouse would need the consent of *both* parents (in other words 'you too') to move abroad. Be prepared for a future relocation. The parent in charge of the children can move anywhere he or she wants to within the UK if it is in their best interest.

Transfer of money or assets

A capital payment to a spouse may have been agreed in your financial settlement and this will need to be paid at the specified time after the divorce is finalised. This may involve releasing funds from deposit accounts or selling/ transferring shares and other assets in order to meet the payment.

Don't forget to look at the tax implications of this payment requirement as it can have a significant effect on the value that you (or your ex-spouse) finally achieve. For example, you may be required to transfer shares to your ex-spouse upon divorce. Transfers of assets between current spouses do not normally create tax charges — but a transfer to or from a person who is no longer your spouse because you are now divorced may do.

Normally, assets transferred between civil partners or spouses in the tax year during which they have lived together, including the year of separation, are exempt from Capital Gains Tax (CGT). However, from the end of the tax year of separation the situation changes and if you have large financial assets to be redistributed then you may want to take this into account. Seek advice on this subject if it affects you.

Careful financial planning and timing are important here. Tax positions and legislation can change regularly and the comments above may already have become out of date by the time you might go through a divorce of your own. Check with your accountant or financial adviser before making any changes to make sure that the legislation has not changed. You don't want to pay tax where you don't need to.

The tax year runs from the 6th April each year to the 5th April the following year, with most individual annual tax allowances being renewed each year. Each individual is taxed separately, so take this into account with your negotiations. Your accountant or financial adviser is best placed to make sure you minimise the effects of tax.

Other less important assets, such as cars, may need to change ownership, and the ownership documents may need to be changed along with your driving licence if you are moving home.

Documents

As suggested earlier in the book, you still need to be able to function once you leave the matrimonial home. You may need your Passport and Driving Licence and you will probably need utility bills as proof of identity. Don't forget your Birth Certificate, Marriage Certificate and Will. Think this through and ensure that you collect what you need if you are 'jumping' so that if the locks get changed when you leave your home, you are not stuck without documentation, being unable to move your life forward.

Paying maintenance

If you have agreed to maintenance payments after the marriage is dissolved, either to your ex-spouse or for child maintenance (or both), then you will need to set these payments up promptly. The reality is that you may have already been paying some form of maintenance and therefore this will be a continuation of the process. It's just the amount you pay that may change.

If you are paying spousal maintenance and also child maintenance, you may want to set up two payments from your bank account so that each payment can be evidenced, rather than merging both payments into one (even if they are being paid to the same bank account) such as your ex-spouse's. This is purely a recording point, but it may make things clearer if there is a dispute at a later date and payments records are required or if maintenance payments are to be adjusted.

Protecting your payments

Maintenance is usually paid by standing order from the payer's bank account, but in certain circumstances it can be capitalised as a single payment to the recipient in advance so that he or she is not reliant on the payment each month. Also, some maintenance payers prefer it this way because it keeps contact to a minimum.

For those who have agreed to pay a regular maintenance payment, they may also be required to take out life assurance cover to protect the maintenance payments if they should die in the early years, leaving a family without income. In certain circumstances one ex-spouse takes out life cover on the other. The insured ex-spouse will have to co-operate as medical underwriting may be required and he or she will need to sign the life assurance application forms and fill in the medical questions required. If the spouse is taking the policy out on the life of the ex-spouse then he or she is insuring 'The life of another'. If the cover levels you require are high, then the medical underwriting may take a little time so make sure that you start the process with time to spare. Most applications can be resolved and completed in around six to eight weeks.

The maintenance receiver pays the premiums for the life cover. This gives the person who receives the maintenance the protection of knowing that the life cover will remain in place and that the premiums required will not stop when no one is looking (or placed in Trust to someone else) because the proceeds will always be paid to the policy owner.

Speak to your financial adviser about the cost of this protection before requesting this as part of your settlement in case the premiums required for the cover are prohibitive. They may also be able to use an existing protection policy, if available and appropriate.

Pension sharing

When you are in the process of getting divorced and are considering the assets of the marriage for division, this will usually include such marital assets as the house, cash, investments and pensions. A pension share can only be achieved by a court order, achieved by the Pension Annex illustrated earlier in Chapter 4.

It would be reasonable at this point to detail how a pension can be split. However, in any interview I provide to a client in a divorce situation, I always pause at this stage to confirm that he or she knows how a pension works because it is easy to make this assumption (especially if the pension was not originally yours). To do the subject justice, I will do the same here.

How a pension works

It is important to understand how a pension works because on some occasions the pension has a greater value than any other asset of the marriage, including the main home. Pensions can be complicated (I should know) with differing factors and rules to individual arrangements. Therefore, for this text, I have tried to keep these notes relatively simple to give a broad overview. Each individual case will need individual advice so speak to a qualified independent financial adviser.

During your lifetime you, your employer and the government may make contributions to a pension fund in your sole name. It is in your sole name for tax purposes, as we will note in a moment. The reason why you or your employer (or both) may pay into a scheme is because it is tax efficient to do so, with tax relief usually being granted on the funds added to your individual pot, or allowing the expense of contributing by giving you (or your employer) tax relief in some other format. Once the money is paid to the scheme, the money is usually invested and (hopefully) grows, either with returns in the investment markets or with accrual notionally allocated to you for future benefit dependent on how much you earn and the number of years you serve in an occupational pension scheme (sometimes called a final salary pension scheme). The value of funds held in investment markets can fall as well as rise.

In the event of your death before retirement, a death benefit is usually paid. This may amount to the value of the fund passed on to your spouse/family, or a percentage of the pension that would have been received had you made it to your normal retirement age.

At the point when you want to retire, you can take a tax free lump sum from the fund and then a taxable income from the remaining balance for the rest of your life, usually purchased from an insurance company. The tax free cash might be around 25 per cent of the fund from a personal pension, and a different calculation is usually applied to a final salary or occupational pension scheme depending on the rules applied to that individual scheme.

To achieve income from the fund after any tax free cash has been paid (if you decide that's what you want) an *Annuity* may be purchased. An annuity is usually a lump sum purchase of income for the balance of your life. The income that the annuity pays is taxable, which is why it is in your sole name at the outset — it can then be taxed in your sole name when being paid to you. When a pension is divided on divorce, the income that is split away will then be paid to your ex-spouse and taxed in *his or her* sole name.

How much income you achieve from your annuity purchase will depend on what you want the annuity to give you. You can protect a spouse, protect against inflation, protect against early death, each providing a different level of initial income. If you have an employer's scheme, the type of income that you will receive may be detailed by the scheme and you should have a pension scheme booklet for this. Your Human Resources department will give you a copy if required. You may want to speak to an independent financial adviser about your options and seek the best annuity rate terms. Many companies offer annuity terms and rates vary, with some being more competitive than others.

Once 'in payment' (in other words, when you have bought a pension annuity) the capital you invested into the annuity is gone. Anyone in poor health can buy an *impaired life annuity,* which can provide a higher level of income at the outset. There are even *smoker annuities,* which provide the potential for higher income, because life expectancy is usually reduced.

You will need to think carefully about the annuity you purchase (or alternative arrangement, such as an Income Drawdown plan) to ensure that it increases if you want to protect against inflation, or wish for it to continue paying to a spouse if you die, or it has a guarantee of payment if you die in the first five or ten years, as examples.

Pension offsetting

When the pension assets of the marriage are being considered, there are various ways of dealing with them, and I have listed examples of these below. For example, you may agree for these pension assets to be *offset*. What does this mean?

Effectively, it means that the value of a pension fund is *offset* against the value of another asset, such as equity in the main home. For instance, one party might keep their pension benefits, but forego a proportion of property equity in order to take account of this benefit. In some cases, parts of a pension have been discounted because they were accrued before the marriage.

As an example, if someone joined a pension scheme at age 24, but only married at age 29, the first five years of the accumulation of benefit may not be added into the calculation for division between the now-divorcing spouses. Exactly how that first five years *is* valued will depend on the type of scheme.

Many legal advisers will currently also consider two approaches to the division of pension assets: by percentage, or based on equality of income.

However, before going into these points it should be noted that if the pension schemes relating to the marriage are complicated or of significant value, as examples, then you may choose to introduce the services of an actuary for actuarial services to provide a calculated value of the real value of a scheme to each spouse, such as final salary scheme. This option may cost more and your solicitor or independent financial adviser may recommend an individual or company to help you with an individual assessment.

Dividing pension assets by percentage

Pension benefits can be divided in a percentage proportion. This can be any amount and may also depend on whether an offset arrangement has been used, as detailed above. A division might be as low as five or ten per cent of the fund, up to 100 per cent of a particular pension pot.

The pension pot value is usually detailed as a *CETV*, which stands for Cash Equivalent Transfer Value. If you run a simple personal pension, then this will be the fund value on the day its benefit is transferred to an ex-spouse, if agreed. If it's a final salary scheme, then the CETV is effectively calculated as a fair value of the current benefits and it should be noted that the actual value to the pension holder may well be higher in terms of the income that it could pay. Some might argue that this is the *cash in value*, rather than the actual value. This may be a good example of where you may need the services of an actuary to see what benefit is being lost by transferring, if at all.

For example, if the pension fund is being split 50/50, and the pension fund value is £100,000, then the final share order in favour of the soon to be ex-spouse will be for 50 per cent of the fund, which should equate to around £50,000. I say *around* £50,000 because all of this process will take time and usually the final fund value will fluctuate over the period before the final day when funds are secured in the other party's name. This can lead to disappointment for some individuals when the investment markets have moved against them at the time of the transfer. Sadly, there is little control to be had over the timing of the transfer and the pension firm has the right to take up to four months to achieve the final transfer from the day they receive all of the necessary paperwork, such as the stamped documents from the court (Decree Absolute and Pension Sharing Annex).

Dividing assets by equality of income

An alternative to this procedure for dividing the pension assets is to base it on equality of income.

I am not an actuary (and as suggested, in some circumstances one may be needed) so this overview has been kept simple to provide a flavour of the process. Let me consider an example, based on current pension annuity purchase rates at the time when this book was written. If a husband of around 60 years old is three years older than his wife, he is likely to have a pension *annuity rate* (the rate used to calculate the pension income) around 10 per cent higher than that of his spouse. This is because he is older and also because, as a male, he is likely to live for a shorter time than his female counterpart.

Taking this into account, to achieve an equitable split of income based on the fund value available is likely to see the division of the pension capital being adjusted with a higher percentage going to the female and a lower amount going to the male because of the variance in the annuity rate. However, please remember that each case is different and many issues can affect the final income, such the ages of each party, fund values and even how the pension fund has been accumulated. This can be a complicated area so seek professional financial advice on this issue, preferably from a qualified financial adviser specialising in pension in divorce or an actuary.

The administration

Pension sharing orders can usually be applied by the spouse in receipt of the Annex to their ex-spouse's pension benefits. These papers normally arrive at around the same time as the *Decree Absolute,* sealed by the court.

The receiving spouse should take independent financial advice on the process of applying the pension sharing order, to secure the benefit for their future. You should also check at the outset how your financial adviser is going to be paid, either by fees, commission or a combination of these options. The existing pension provider may make a charge to undertake this transfer work and this will usually have to be paid in advance. If the costs for this transfer are split equally between both parties (which in my professional experience has happened often) then your ex-spouse will also need to pay his or her share. Some ex-spouses can be reluctant to pay their percentage of the fees, 50 per cent as an example, and this can delay things, although they are required to pay. In some cases the costs can be deducted from the fund, if required and allowed by the scheme.

For older divorcing couples, part of the divorce settlement may include the need to draw pension benefits as soon as they are transferred. The minimum retirement age available to draw pension benefits is now 55 (from 6th April 2010) recently increased from 50. Many recipients of pension benefits are not aware of this and the fact that the pension income available is taxable. It's essential to get advice on these pension issues before the settlement is finalised, so that all participants' expectations are managed.

For older divorcing couples, it should be noted that most pensions in payment, and by that I mean when the pension owner is receiving income and has taken tax free cash if that is what they are going to do, can still be divided for divorce purposes by a Pension Sharing Order . This may well be significant for those who are divorcing in later life.

Basic State Pension

You might want to consider the benefits available to each party from the Basic State Pension. There are usually two types of state pension that may be accrued, namely the *Basic State Pension* and *the State Earnings Related Pension*) (SERPS) or *Second State Pension*) (S2P) as it is now called. This may be particularly relevant if the divorce happens close to the end of a working life.

Most people are entitled to some form of state pension at any age from 60 for women and from 65 for men. The minimum age for the state pension is equalising for all to age 65, and then this is likely to increase in stages to age 68 in future years.

The benefits available can be checked by completing a *BR19 State Pension Forecast* form, which will tell you what you are entitled to, both now and in the future. Your spouse should also be entitled to individual pension benefits.

On divorce, there is the potential to transfer some of the State Pension Benefits to your ex-spouse dependent on your circumstances and this may be required as part of a divorce settlement. To find out the transfer value of any benefit you can request this information from The Pension Service in Newcastle using an original *BR20 form*, one for each party. They don't like photocopies and the valuation is valid for twelve months.

Both the BR19 Pension Forecast Form and the BR20 Form are available on The Pension Service website, www.thepensionservice.gov.uk.

Whether or not you are divorcing, it's always worth checking your State Pension to make sure you are maximising the pension benefit that could be available to you. For married couples, I would usually recommend that both parties check to ensure that the household will benefit from this income.

Currently the income from the State Pension is paid gross to the recipient, but is taxable. This may mean that any other income you receive above the State Pension has a greater tax charge to take account of the State Pension already in payment.

Contribution records and State Pension Benefits after divorce

When a divorce is finalised and completed, you can re-check the State Pension benefits available to you, to see whether they have changed. You may see an increase in your benefits if your spouse's National Insurance contribution record was higher than yours as they may use this record as a substitute. Again, you can use a BR19 form for this, updated with the concluded changes, such as the fact that your marital status is now 'divorced' and the date of the divorce. The response will usually be with you in around a month's time, however the time taken can vary.

Notes/ Questions to ask?

Notes/ Questions to ask?

6. Recovery

Many people find the indignity and insult of getting divorced to be a heavy burden. It represents an admittance that something has failed or gone wrong. For example, if one person has committed adultery, was that because they are by nature a philanderer, or because their spouse did not pay enough attention? Or was it just because one party thought that they could get away with it and got caught? It may not be as simple as that, but these factors will usually affect how you feel at every stage of the process.

At the end of the divorce proceedings, no one is ever left with absolutely nothing. However there are some people who feel that *is* the case.

When you form a marriage union, you are doing so usually for love and companionship and for how each party can enhance the other's life. In other words, what they can *add,* rather than *take.* Each party will usually experience the same, which is why you both agreed to the marriage in the first place. That might seem a bit simplistic and probably is, but there is some truth in there.

There *is* life after divorce, however difficult it is to believe in the heat of battle. You should expect to have to dig deep to start the process of recovery, however.

For many people, it is certainly a financial adjustment. In some cases the adjustment is for the better, but for many people it means starting again at a lower financial point than they are used to. This re-start may take some adjustment (both emotionally and financially), depending on the circumstances. The issue of when or whether to start dating/socialising again, as an example, can also seem daunting, to say the least.

Some divorcees never fully recover from the effects and loss of a marriage. It is like bereavement, but no one has passed away. This is why you should expect any recovery to take time. Even someone who is leaving the marriage for a new partner has usually lost a friend. They may well still miss what they once shared together and reflect fondly on the good times. Those who are starting out on their own again will have similar feelings, although they may not have the comfort of someone to share them with.

As with any good financial planning, you need to start early in your personal planning for your emotional and physical future. From an emotional point of view, security may be the key to your well being. You have decided where you are going to live (and possibly also with whom) and you may well still be seeing your ex-spouse because of contact with the children. On the contact point, parties will need to be mature about this process. Some people even go as far as to apply a business philosophy to the process, detaching from their emotions to see them through. Grandparents are likely to wish to remain involved in their grandchildren's lives and will continue to aim to see their heirs (and you) regularly. It can seem surreal at times, with everyone trying to get along now that the fighting has stopped. But life must go on and the sooner this is adjusted to, the better.

Divorce does not mean that you will never see the ex-spouse again, especially if you have children. You may have to pick up the children from their new home, even have them handed over to you by your ex-spouse's new partner or the children's grandparents (your old in-laws)— and maturity and respect will be the name of the game here. This may not mean that you have seen the last of the disagreements, if these collection arrangements ever go wrong.

From a financial point of view, you need to budget quickly to take account of any new (or continued) outgoings, such as rent, a new mortgage liability or maintenance payments, either being paid or being paid to you. You may have also received a capital payment that will need to be invested for your future rebuilding requirements. Don't forget the basic financial planning suggestions, which are:

- Keep three to six months' income as an emergency deposit fund for immediate cash needs

- Don't hold too much money with one deposit provider in case they go wrong, as we have witnessed in recent times

- Consider re-writing your Will to reflect your changed circumstances and update your pension death nominations

- Keep up to date with any payments you have agreed, to ensure you keep your credit rating positive

This all sounds very straightforward. However, the reality may be that in achieving all this planning, you may be left with little money to fund your own lifestyle.

Getting a close handle on your weekly and monthly costs early can be the difference between sinking and swimming. Take into account new travel costs if you are now travelling further to work or travelling to collect, ferry around and deliver children. This might even mean having to buy a new vehicle to ensure that the car makes it there and back safely. If this is in question then make sure that you sign up to some form of breakdown service. (And I am not referring to an emotional breakdown service!)

How long is your emotional recovery going to take? Three months? Six months? Two years? Make sure you plan accordingly because for many people 'recovery' means *survival*. For others, it is the beginning of a new era, almost a cleansing process, and an exciting opportunity away from the burdens of the previous incumbent. This may be the reason why you decided to divorce in the first place. However, you will always discover something hanging around your house that reminds you of your past. It is inevitable.

But the day will come when it is all over and you must and will recover. Are you ready for your new start? If not, then start planning what you *really* want to happen in your future.

Discovery

No, I don't mean the 4x4 you used to have before the divorce!

It is going to be difficult to recover if you have not discovered what (if anything) was wrong with what you did in the first place. I hope that you are not going to suggest that you were completely innocent and that the breakdown of the previous marriage was all the fault of the other long-departed spouse. I know that I have been on a journey of self-discovery throughout and subsequently following the divorce processes. This probably all seems a bit too late, but it is only by going through the divorce process that you may come out the other side realising that some of your own mannerisms, personal style and attitude may not be what they should be.

It is interesting that many older couples are now getting divorced, as they approach the next phase of their lives, usually leading into retirement and the autumn years of their time. Having nurtured a family, they then reach a point where they have to make decisions on the direction that their lives should take. Some decide that they would prefer to go their different ways because they have lived up until now for the children or their work, and this is now coming to its climax and end.

It used to be said that life begins at 40. In my view, this was based on the fact that life expectancy used to be around 70-75. Now, with the general public living until 80 or more, life probably starts at 55. And many people decide to start again with a clean sheet at this time of life. Some will disagree with these thoughts. A good friend of mine suggests that for him, it definitely starts at age 40 and he does not think this is related to life expectancy. He feels that it is to do with confidence and sagacity.

'In your teens and twenties you spend all your time trying to impress others. In your thirties, you are still trying to do this as well as build up wealth and a family. In your forties, you realise that living to impress others is pointless', he said.

My friend believes that you then become confident in your own skin and realise that your wisdom and experience enables you to gain the respect of others without needing to try to impress. This allows you to start living your own life the way you want to and not how you feel that others would want you to live your life.

Fulfilment is not a word I use often and one I am not sure I have achieved. But what does *fulfilment* mean to you and, probably more importantly, what does it mean to your spouse or partner? What do you each want from your union? And if you really think you know, when was the last time you checked their understanding, and they checked yours?

This might just be basic marital communication. And if it is nothing more than that, do make sure that you don't lose this fundamental gift amongst the noise and bustle of our busy modern lives.

Consider what it was that went wrong for you. How did it happen? Did it just creep up on you over the years, so that before you knew it you were alone, at least emotionally? Whatever you do, don't feel embarrassed at what has happened, as many people do. Understanding and learning from the issues is important for your own well being — but dwelling on them is not. If you are finding it difficult to adjust to this new format in your life then you may want to seek counselling to help alleviate the situation. Again, you may want to contact Relate or speak to your doctor.

Remember what I said about being a *divorce bore*. Don't start being one now, when it's all over.

It's time to move on with your life and to start again.

Notes/ Questions to ask?

7. Planning to start again

When you divorce, it does not mean that you lose all the *values* that you brought to the original marriage in the first place. It may mean that those two parties no longer share those *values* anymore. You are still funny, intelligent, bold, beautiful, strong, and enthusiastic. Whatever you were before, you have not lost it. So, after the divorce you will be set free to start your new life.

You might decide to move location or work or both! Divorce can and should be considered as a 'life junction' where you are free to decide which way you want your life to go from now on, and in what format. This is a great opportunity. You might be on your own or with a new partner, but wherever you find yourself, it is up to you to shape your life your way. It is your responsibility now, no one else's, and a whole new world opens up to you.

I know that many people dislike change, especially this sort, but divorce is a change that usually cannot be anticipated and, once the ball starts rolling, it will not usually stop until the process is completed. So, change is coming and it has your name on it.

Some people decide that living alone is the best and only option for the immediate future. The niche 'divorced' singles market has created significant demand in various sectors, including housing and travel. There has been a boom in one and two-bedroomed properties and the 'singles' market for holidays is significant. Many people find the 'single' option the path of least resistance, believing 'once bitten twice shy'. There are also people who simply can't face the potential indignity of things going wrong all over again in years to come.

If you have 'you', at least you can rely on 'you'. You have everything, rather than nothing. The world could easily be your oyster, it is a question of what you're going to do about it.

At this point I can offer you only limited help. We are all individuals with unique needs and desires. All I would say is follow the route that you believe to be true for you, and you are unlikely to be disappointed.

Race to the altar

Life does not stand still and you may find yourself in another relationship before long, or even immediately if that was the cause of the original break-up. Don't forget that, once you are released from the marriage contract, so is your ex-spouse. With a *Decree Absolute*, some people go right ahead and marry straight after their divorce. If your ex-spouse finds new love and marriage, you will find out quickly from one source or another. You may be very pleased about this, but many people find this difficult to adjust to at first.

Financial planning for you and a new partner

This brings to mind some of the financial planning points that you might want to consider to ensure you are protecting your loved ones, whether they be from the past or in the future.

These points could apply whether you have been married before and are starting out with a partner for the first time, or like me, you have a bit of 'mileage on the clock' and are planning within another relationship.

Wills

If you are going to live with someone for a long period, or perhaps marry in the future, do check that both you and he or she are protected. Make sure that you both make Wills, noting who gets what. Also check that the nomination on death benefits under a private or employer's pension, and death in service schemes, are up to date to reflect your circumstances.

Wills are revoked on marriage, unless they were set up specifically in contemplation of marriage. Therefore, if you do decide to tie the knot after a long period, then you will need to update your Wills to reflect this new marriage contract.

Wills are also affected on divorce. If you had nominated a spouse to be your executor or trustee, then he or she will be treated as having died on the date when the marriage was dissolved. Also, any property or interest in property that had been bequeathed shall pass as if the former spouse had died on the date to which the marriage was dissolved — unless there is a statement to the contrary in the Will. Clearly, divorce will affect the outcome of the Will. You may want to nominate your children or new partner. Whatever you do, ensure that the document is kept safe and up to date.

You may also want to ensure that someone you trust knows where the Will document is kept, so it can be found quickly to ensure that your assets are distributed in the way you would want them.

Cohabiting

Many couples cohabit before they marry (whether they are marrying for the first time or remarrying). In the world we live in, this may be the only real way of finding out what a person is truly like before they take the marriage plunge.

If you have bought a house together, a deposit may have been found and, usually, a mortgage secured to fund the purchase price. You move in together and suddenly the world is a happy place, up to your neck in DIY brochures and cans of emulsion. But if one of you dies, who owns the deceased's part of the house if there is no Will? Assuming you are the surviving partner, it is not necessarily you who will inherit the house. It is possible for it to be a dependant or relative of the deceased, such as their parents or children. If you don't fancy owning a house jointly with your loved one's parents as an example, then make a Will.

Also, you may have put different deposit levels into the purchase. Until you know that you are really going to spend the rest of your lives together, you can arrange for the house to be owned as 'tenants in common' (rather than 'joint tenants') specifying a clear division or percentage of who owns what proportion of the new property. Speak to your solicitor or legal adviser about this point and he or she will guide you accordingly.

Death benefits and nominations

What happens to your pension if you die before being awarded the 'gold watch' at retirement? Surely the fund does not disappear when you have still been adding to it? No it doesn't, although it may well disappear once you pass your chosen retirement age.

When you completed your application form to start a personal pension or an employer's pension scheme, you should have been asked to nominate who you want to get your benefits if you die before the age of 60 or 65, whichever applied to you at the time. If you started young with your retirement planning you may have nominated your parents, and if you were a little older you may have nominated your long term partner at the time. So, what does your pension nomination say now? Have you checked recently?

Professionally, I have suffered one or two embarrassing moments when information about a pension comes back to me for a couple, and at the point where it details a 'death nomination' it has the name of a 'beau' from the past. Saying that, in another case it detailed another partner altogether and I had to discreetly ask the individual who that person was? A mistress was revealed and quickly removed from the document at the request of the client.

If you have previously nominated a spouse and have now started the process of going your separate ways, you can contact your pension provider or your employer's Human Resources department to change the nomination. Making this change usually costs nothing, and it can be as simple as providing a letter. However, before you do any of this, think carefully. You may have been contributing to the household bills and your responsibility for the costs of the household may not end just because your marriage or civil partnership is over.

You will have to decide who is nominated, and how the costs of the household are going to be met if one party lives elsewhere whilst the separation is proceeding. Also, if you were to die during the course of any divorce proceedings, then the family would still need to be protected and the children would still need a roof over their heads. Bear this in mind when updating any nomination.

You will survive

Having experienced many of the divorce issues detailed in this text twice, I can vouch for the fact that there *is* life after divorce, although there were many times when it was difficult to see any light at the end of the legal tunnel. However, here I am writing this book, happily married again and therefore I must have survived.

Divorce was always going to be a time of change and possibly turmoil, if not upheaval, for those parties involved. This applies whether they were voluntarily part of the process or not, such as the children of the marriage. Recent statistics show that in 2008 there were 60,806 children involved in 121,779 marriages that were dissolved in the year. (source: Office of National Statistics).

For me, on many occasions, it was the uncertainty of the process and the potential outcomes that caused me the greatest anxiety and the most sleepless nights. Each element of the process detailed in this book needs the relevant attention paid to it, to achieve a suitable outcome. It will certainly guide you to what happens next.

This book has been designed to help with details of what needs to be considered during the divorce process. However, do remember that each divorce and settlement will be different because each marriage (and the assets of each marriage) will be unique. I hope also that these notes may give you some food for thought about the way you might approach any final agreement, if at all. You may even have decided that this is all too much to take on, and that you will give your union another go to see if all this change can be avoided. The choice is yours.

Assuming you do decide that you will start or continue through the divorce process, then remember that all of the parties (family, grandparents and true friends) that are involved, and who still care for you and the family, may suffer upheaval

If you have children, then place them at the forefront of your actions to make sure that they have the security and love that they have come to enjoy from the past. However hard it is, this will help them in the future, even if it does not help you now. They will need their routines, their leisure time, attention, education and full participation from both parents and the grandparents. Don't forget the grandparents (however awkward they may be) because they will savour the opportunity of being with their grandchildren, even if the children's parents are no longer together. It is important to consider the effects from the grandparent's viewpoint. After all, it is possible that they lose contact with your spouse, a relative with whom they might have been very friendly. Most importantly they only have limited rights to gain contact with their grandchildren, which may be the most precious things in their lives. Grandparents are entitled to ask the court for leave to apply for contact with their grandchildren if this cannot be resolved amicably.

In this emotional rollercoaster, behaving with maturity and respect seems to be the best route for all parties to enable a smooth transition through divorce. Maturity certainly has the potential of keeping the costs down, although the reality of events may overtake an individual's ability to apply such qualities.

However, when it boils down to it, this is a legal process and dissolution of a marriage contract between two parties with various advisers in the middle. It will all take time to resolve once started. Remember, it is your life and only *you* know how *you* want to live it and with whom.

You decide your future, take good advice, and I hope that the result turns out the way you wanted it. Eventually, only you will know this.

Most divorcees survive intact, but some are not unscathed by the experience. Poorer and hopefully now wiser, many would argue that people change during the divorce process; that they become hardened to life's twists and turns, and cool to many emotional situations that they would have once embraced.

I suggest on the back cover of this book that divorce is a rather hollow experience and that any victories along the way will be shallow and short lived. I still believe this.

As for the solicitors, as with any industry or profession, there are some real stars, quality professionals that will really help you through without billing you at every opportunity. I am privileged to know a few locally in Guildford. Sadly, as with all professions, there are others who will act differently.

All you can do is prepare yourself for your journey of divorce, if you plan to take one. I hope this book has given you greater insight into the overall process and its possible wrinkles. Your situation will be different to others because you are different, but at least you now know the framework through which divorce may lead you. You are likely to falter at some stage on the way, and this will need to be overcome to get to the next stage, so the sooner it is faced the better.

Overall, you will still have 'you' and the values that you have always held. Divorce can never take those values away from you and you will see that soon, I promise.

Notes/ Questions to ask?

Appendix:
The Financial Statement / Form E

FINANCIAL STATEMENT OF

In the	*[Principal Registry of the Family ... Court]
Case No.	
*[Petitioner's/Applicant's solicitor's reference]	*[delete as appropriate]
*[Respondent's solicitor's reference]	

[Husband][Wife]*[Civil partner]

Between

and

Who is the *[husband]*[wife]*[civil partner]
[Petitioner][Respondent] in the
[divorce][dissolution] suit

Applicant in this matter

Who is the *[husband]*[wife]*[civil partner]
[Petitioner][Respondent] in the
[divorce][dissolution] suit

Respondent in this matter

Please fill in this form fully and accurately. Where any box is not applicable, write 'N/A'.

You have a duty to the court to give a full, frank and clear disclosure of all your financial and other relevant circumstances.

A failure to give full and accurate disclosure may result in any order the court makes being set aside.

If you are found to have been deliberately untruthful, criminal proceedings for perjury may be taken against you.

You must attach documents to the form where they are specifically sought and you may attach other documents where it is necessary to explain or clarify any of the information that you give.

Essential documents that must accompany this statement are detailed in the form.

If there is not enough room on the form for any particular piece of information, you may continue on an attached sheet of paper.

If you are in doubt about how to complete any part of this form you should seek legal advice.

The statement must be sworn before a solicitor, a commissioner for oaths or an Officer of the Court duly authorised official, before it is filed with the Court or sent to the other party (see fee note page)

This statement is filed by

Name and address of solicitor

...E Financial Statement (12.06)

FINANCIAL STATEMENT

OF

	In the
	*[High/County Court]
	*[Principal Registry of the Family Division]
	Case No. Always quote this
	Petitioner's Solicitor's reference
	Respondent's Solicitor's reference

*Husband/*Wife/*Civil partner

*(*delete as appropriate)*

Between

		and	

Who is the *husband/*wife/*civil partner
*Petitioner/*Respondent in the
*divorce/*dissolution suit

Applicant in this matter

Who is the *husband/*wife/*civil partner
*Petitioner/*Respondent in the
*divorce/*dissolution suit

Respondent in this matter

Please fill in this form fully and accurately. Where any box is not applicable, write 'N/A'.

You have a duty to the court to give a full, frank and clear disclosure of all your financial and other relevant circumstances.

A failure to give full and accurate disclosure may result in any order the court makes being set aside.

If you are found to have been deliberately untruthful, criminal proceedings for perjury may be taken against you.

You must attach documents to the form where they are specifically sought and you may attach other documents where it is necessary to explain or clarify any of the information that you give.

Essential documents that must accompany this statement are detailed in the form.

If there is not enough room on the form for any particular piece of information, you may continue on an attached sheet of paper.

If you are in doubt about how to complete any part of this form you should seek legal advice.

This Statement must be sworn before a solicitor, a commissioner for oaths or an Officer of the Court or, if abroad, a notary or duly authorised official, before it is filed with the Court or sent to the other party (see last page).

This statement is filed by

Name and address of solicitor

Form E Financial Statement (12.05)

HMCS

1 General Information

1.1 Full name

1.2 Date of birth

Date	Month	Year

1.3 Date of the marriage/ civil partnership

Date	Month	Year

1.4 Occupation

1.5 Date of the separation

Date	Month	Year

Tick here if not applicable ☐

1.6 Date of the

Petition			Decree nisi/Decree of judicial separation/ Conditional order/ Separation order			Decree absolute/ Final order (if applicable)		
Date	Month	Year	Date	Month	Year	Date	Month	Year

1.7 If you have subsequently married or formed a civil partnership, or will do so, state the date

Date	Month	Year

1.8 Are you co-habiting? Yes ☐ No ☐

1.9 Do you intend to co-habit within the next six months? Yes ☐ No ☐

1.10 Details of any children of the family

Full names	Date of birth			With whom does the child live?
	Date	Month	Year	

1.11 Details of the state of health of yourself and the children, if you think this should be taken into account

Yourself	Children

2

© **Crown copyright**

1.12 Details of the present and proposed future educational arrangements for the children.

Present arrangements	Future arrangements

1.13 Details of any child support maintenance calculation or any maintenance order or agreement made in respect of any children of the family. If no calculation, order or agreement has been made, give an estimate of the liability of the non-resident parent in respect of the children of the family under the Child Support Act 1991.

1.14 If this application is to vary an order, attach a copy of the order and give details of the part that is to be varied and the changes sought. You may need to continue on a separate sheet.

1.15 Details of any other court cases between you and your spouse/civil partner, whether in relation to money, property, children or anything else.

Case No	Court

1.16 Your present residence and the occupants of it and on what terms you occupy it (e.g. tenant, owner-occupier).

Address	Occupants	Terms of occupation

2 Financial Details *Part I Real Property and Personal Assets*

2.1 Complete this section in respect of the family home (the last family home occupied by you and your spouse/civil partner) if it remains unsold.

Documentation required for attachment to this section:

a) A copy of any valuation of the property obtained within the last six months. If you cannot provide this document, please give your own realistic estimate of the current market value

b) A recent mortgage statement confirming the sum outstanding on **each** mortgage

Property name and address	
Land Registry title number	
Mortgage company name(s) and address(es) and account number(s)	
Type of mortgage	
Details of who owns the property and the extent of your legal and beneficial interest in it (i.e. state if it is owned by you solely or jointly owned with your spouse/civil partner or with others)	
If you consider that the legal ownership as recorded at the Land Registry does not reflect the true position, state why	
Current market value of the property	
Balance outstanding on any mortgage(s)	
If a sale at this stage would result in penalties payable under the mortgage, state amount	
Estimate the costs of sale of the property	
Total equity in the property (i.e. market value less outstanding mortgage(s), penalties if any and the costs of sale)	
TOTAL value of your interest in the family home: Total A	£

4

2.2 **Details of your interest in any other property, land or buildings. Complete one page for each property you have an interest in.**

Documentation required for attachment to this section:

a) A copy of any valuation of the property obtained within the last six months. If you cannot provide this document, please give your own realistic estimate of the current market value

b) A recent mortgage statement confirming the sum outstanding on each mortgage

Property name and address	
Land Registry title number	
Mortgage company name(s) and address(es) and account number(s)	
Type of mortgage	
Details of who owns the property and the extent of your legal and beneficial interest in it (i.e. state if it is owned by you solely or jointly owned with your spouse/civil partner or with others)	
If you consider that the legal ownership as recorded at the Land Registry does not reflect the true position, state why	
Current market value of the property	
Balance outstanding on any mortgage(s)	
If a sale at this stage would result in penalties payable under the mortgage, state amount	
Estimate the costs of sale of the property	
Total equity in the property (i.e. market value less outstanding mortgage(s), penalties if any and the costs of sale)	
Total value of your interest in this property	
TOTAL value of your interest in ALL other property: Total B	£

5

© **Crown copyright**

2.5 Details of all life insurance policies including endowment policies that you hold or have an interest in. Include those that do not have a surrender value. Complete one page for each policy.

Documentation required for attachment to this section:
A surrender valuation of each policy that has a surrender value.

Name of company			
Policy type			
Policy number			
If policy is assigned, state in whose favour and amount of charge			
Name of any other owner and the extent of your interest in the policy			
Maturity date *(if applicable)*	**Date**	**Month**	**Year**
Current surrender value *(if applicable)*			
If policy includes life insurance, the amount of the insurance and the name of the person whose life is insured			
Total current surrender value of your interest in this policy			
TOTAL value of your interest in ALL policies: (C3)	£		

2.6 Details of all monies that are OWED TO YOU. Do not include sums owed in director's or partnership accounts which should be included at section 2.11.

Brief description of money owed and by whom	Balance outstanding	Total current value of your interest
TOTAL value of your interest in ALL debts owed to you: (C4) £		0.00

7

2.7 Details of all cash sums held in excess of £500. You must state where it is held and the currency it is held in.

Where held	Amount	Currency	Total current value of your interest

TOTAL value of your interest in ALL cash sums: (C5) £   0.00

2.8 Details of personal belongings individually worth more than £500.

INCLUDE:
- Cars (gross value)
- Collections, pictures and jewellery
- Furniture and house contents

Brief description of item	Total current value of your interest

TOTAL value of your interest in ALL personal belongings: (C6) £

Add together all the figures in boxes C1 to C6 to give the TOTAL current value of your interest in personal assets: TOTAL C £   0.00

8

© Crown copyright

2 Financial Details *Part 2 Capital: Liabilities and Capital Gains Tax*

2.9 Details of any liabilities you have.

EXCLUDE liabilities already shown such as:
* Mortgages
* Any overdrawn bank, building society or National Savings accounts

INCLUDE:
* Money owed on credit cards and store cards
* Bank loans
* Hire purchase agreements

List all credit and store cards held including those with a nil or positive balance. Where the liability is not solely your own, give the name(s) of the other account holder(s) and the amount of your share of the liability.

Liability	Name(s) of other account holder(s) (if applicable)	Total liability	Total current value of your interest in the liability
TOTAL value of your interest in ALL liabilities: (D1) £			

2.10 If any Capital Gains Tax would be payable on the disposal now of any of your real property or personal assets, give your estimate of the tax liability.

Asset	Total Capital Gains Tax liability
TOTAL value of ALL your potential Capital Gains Tax liabilities: (D2) £	
Add together D1 and D2 to give the TOTAL value of your liabilities: TOTAL D £	0.00

9

2 Financial Details *Part 3 Capital: Business assets and directorships*

2.11 Details of all your business interests. Complete one page for each business you have an interest in.

Documentation required for attachment to this section:
a) Copies of the business accounts for the last two financial years
b) Any documentation, if available at this stage, upon which you have based your estimate of the current value of your interest in this business, for example a letter from an accountant or a formal valuation. It is not essential to obtain a formal valuation at this stage

Name of the business	
Briefly describe the nature of the business	
Are you *(Please delete all those that are not applicable)*	a) Sole trader b) Partner in a partnership with others c) Shareholder in a limited company
If you are a partner or a shareholder, state the extent of your interest in the business (i.e. partnership share or the extent of your shareholding compared to the overall shares issued)	
State when your next set of accounts will be available	
If any of the figures in the last accounts are not an accurate reflection of the current position, state why. For example, if there has been a material change since the last accounts, or if the valuations of the assets are not a true reflection of their value (e.g. because property or other assets have not been re-valued in recent years or because they are shown at a book value)	
Total amount of any sums owed to you by the business by way of a director's loan account, partnership capital or current accounts or the like. Identify where these appear in the business accounts	
Your estimate of the current value of your business interest. Explain briefly the basis upon which you have reached that figure	
Your estimate of any Capital Gains Tax that would be payable if you were to dispose of your business now	
Net value of your interest in this business after any Capital Gains Tax liability	
TOTAL value of ALL your interests in business assets: TOTAL E	£

10

2.12 List any directorships you hold or have held in the last 12 months (other than those already disclosed in Section 2.11).

2 Financial Details *Part 4 Capital: Pensions*

2.13 Give details of all your pension rights. Complete a separate page for each pension.

EXCLUDE:
* Basic State Pension

INCLUDE (complete a separate page for each one):
* Additional State Pension (SERPS and State Second Pension (S2P))
* Free Standing Additional Voluntary Contribution Schemes (FSAVC) separate from the scheme of your employer
* Membership of ALL pension plans or schemes

Documentation required for attachment to this section:

a) A recent statement showing the cash equivalent transfer value (CETV) provided by the trustees or managers of each pension arrangement (or, in the case of the additional state pension, a valuation of these rights)

b) If any valuation is not available, give the estimated date when it will be available and attach a copy of your letter to the pension company or administrators from whom the information was sought and/or state the date on which an application for a valuation of a State Earnings Related Pension Scheme was submitted to the Department of Work and Pensions

Name and address of pension arrangement	
Your National Insurance Number	
Number of pension arrangement or reference number	
Type of scheme e.g. occupational or personal, final salary, money purchase, additional state pension or other (if other, please give details)	
Date the CETV was calculated	
Is the pension in payment or drawdown or deferment? *(Please answer Yes or No)*	
State the cash equivalent transfer value (CETV) quotation, or in the additional state pension, the valuation of those rights	
If the arrangement is an occupational pension arrangement that is paying reduced CETVs, please quote what the CETV would have been if not reduced. If this is not possible, please indicate if the CETV quoted is a reduced CETV	
TOTAL value of ALL your pension assets: TOTAL F	£

12

2 Financial Details *Part 5 Capital: Other assets*

2.14 Give details of any other assets not listed in Parts 1 to 4 above.

INCLUDE (the following list is not exhaustive):
- Any personal or business assets not yet disclosed
- Unrealisable assets
- Share option schemes, stating the estimated net sale proceeds of the shares if the options were capable of exercise now, and whether Capital Gains Tax or income tax would be payable
- Business expansion schemes
- Futures
- Commodities
- Trust interests (including interests under a discretionary trust), stating your estimate of the value of the interest and when it is likely to become realisable. If you say it will never be realisable, or has no value, give your reasons
- Any asset that is likely to be received in the foreseeable future
- Any asset held on your behalf by a third party
- Any asset not disclosed elsewhere on this form even if held outside England and Wales

You are reminded of your obligation to disclose all your financial assets and interests of ANY nature.

Type of asset	Value	Total NET value of your interest
TOTAL value of ALL your other assets: TOTAL G	£	

13

2 Financial Details *Part 6 Income: Earned income from employment*

2.15 Details of earned income from employment. Complete one page for each employment.

Documentation required for attachment to this section:

a) P60 for the last financial year (you should have received this from your employer shortly after the last 5th April)

b) Your last three payslips

c) Your last Form P11D if you have been issued with one

Name and address of your employer	
Job title and brief details of the type of work you do	
Hours worked per week in this employment	
How long have you been with this employer?	
Explain the basis of your income i.e. state whether it is based on an annual salary or an hourly rate of pay and whether it includes commissions or bonuses	
Gross income for the last financial year as shown on your P60	
Net income for the last financial year i.e. gross income less income tax and national insurance	
Average net income for the last three months i.e. total income less income tax and national insurance divided by three	
Briefly explain any other entries on the attached payslips other than basic income, income tax and national insurance	
If the payslips attached for the last three months are not an accurate reflection of your normal income briefly explain why	
Details and value of any bonuses or other occasional payments that you receive from this employment not otherwise already shown, including the basis upon which they are paid	
Details and value of any benefits in kind, perks or other remuneration received from this employer in the last year (e.g. provision of a car, payment of travel, accommodation, meal expenses, etc.)	
Your estimate of your net income from this employment for the next 12 months. If this differs significantly from your current income explain why in box 4.1.2	

Estimated TOTAL of ALL net earned income from employment for the next 12 months: TOTAL H £ _____

14

2 Financial Details *Part 7 Income: Income from self-employment or partnership*

2.16 You will have already given details of your business and provided the last two years accounts at section 2.11. Complete this section giving details of your income from your business. Complete one page for each business.

Documentation required for attachment to this section:

a) A copy of your last tax assessment or, if that is not available, a letter from your accountant confirming your tax liability

b) If net income from the last financial year and estimated net income for the next 12 months is significantly different, a copy of management accounts for the period since your last account

Name of the business	
Date to which your last accounts were completed	
Your share of gross business profit from the last completed accounts	
Income tax and national insurance payable on your share of gross business profit above	
Net income for that year (using the two figures directly above, gross business profit less income tax and national insurance payable)	
Details and value of any benefits in kind, perks or other remuneration received from this business in the last year e.g. provision of a car, payment of travel, accommodation, meal expenses, etc.	
Amount of any regular monthly or other drawings that you take from this business	
If the estimated figure directly below is different from the net income as at the end date of the last completed accounts, briefly explain the reason(s)	
Your estimate of your net annual income for the next 12 months	
Estimated TOTAL of ALL net income from self-employment or partnership for the next 12 months: TOTAL 1	£

15

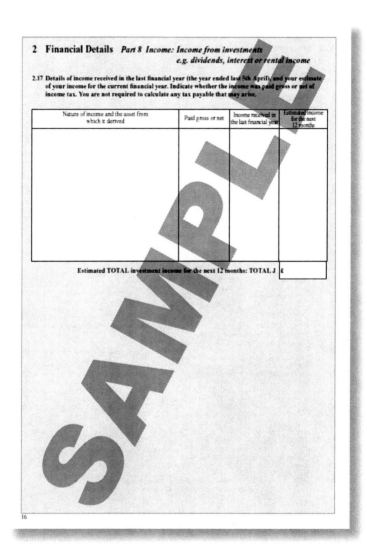

2   Financial Details   *Part 8 Income: Income from investments*
e.g. dividends, interest or rental income

2.17 Details of income received in the last financial year (the year ended last 5th April), and your estimate of your income for the current financial year. Indicate whether the income was paid gross or net of income tax. You are not required to calculate any tax payable that may arise.

Nature of income and the asset from which it derived	Paid gross or net	Income received in the last financial year	Estimated income for the next 12 months
Estimated TOTAL investment income for the next 12 months: TOTAL J			£

16

© **Crown copyright**

2   Financial Details   *Part 9 Income: Income from state benefits (including state pension and child benefit)*

2.18 Details of all state benefits that you are currently receiving.

Name of benefit	Amount paid	Frequency of payment	Estimated income for the next 12 months
Estimated TOTAL benefit income for the next 12 months: TOTAL K			£

17

2   Financial Details   *Part 10   Income: Any other income*

2.19 Details of any other income not disclosed above.

INCLUDE:
- Any source from which income has been received during the last 12 months (even if it has now ceased)
- Any source from which income is likely to be received during the next 12 months

You are reminded of your obligation to give full disclosure of your financial circumstances.

Nature of income	Paid gross or net	Income received in the last financial year	Estimated income for the next 12 months
Estimated TOTAL other income for the next 12 months: TOTAL L			£

18

2 Financial Details *Summaries*

2.20 Summary of your capital (Parts 1 to 5).

Description	Reference of the section on this statement	Value
Current value of your interest in the family home	A	
Current value of your interest in all other property	B	
Current value of your interest in personal assets	C	
Current value of your liabilities	D	
Current value of your interest in business assets	E	
Current value of your pension assets	F	
Current value of all your other assets	G	
TOTAL value of your assets (Totals A to G less D): £		0.00

2.21 Summary of your estimated income for the next 12 months (Parts 6 to 10).

Description	Reference of the section on this statement	Value
Estimated net total of income from employment	H	
Estimated net total of income from self-employment or partnership	I	
Estimated net total of investment income	J	
Estimated state benefit receipts	K	
Estimated net total of all other income	L	
Estimated TOTAL income for the next 12 months (Totals H to L): £		0.00

3 Financial Requirements *Part 1 Income needs*

3.1 Income needs for yourself and for any children living with you or provided for by you. ALL figures should be annual, monthly or weekly (state which). You *must not* use a combination of these periods. State your current income needs and, if these are likely to change in the near future, explain the anticipated change and give an estimate of the future cost.

The income needs below are: *(delete those not applicable)*	Weekly	Monthly	Annual

I anticipate my income needs are going to change because

3.1.1 Income needs for yourself.

INCLUDE:
- All income needs for yourself
- Income needs for any children living with you or provided for by you only if these form part of your total income needs (e.g. housing, fuel, car expenses, holidays, etc)

Item	Current cost	Estimated future cost
	SUB-TOTAL your income needs: £	

3.1.2 Income needs for children living with you or provided for by you.

INCLUDE:
- Only those income needs that are different to those of your household shown above

Item	Current cost	Estimated future cost
	SUB-TOTAL children's income needs: £	
	TOTAL of ALL income needs: £	0.00

20

3 Financial Requirements *Part 2 Capital needs*

3.2 Set out below the reasonable future capital needs for yourself and for any children living with you or provided for by you.

3.2.1 Capital needs for yourself.

INCLUDE:
- All capital needs for yourself
- Capital needs for any children living with you or provided for by you only if these form part of your total capital needs (e.g. housing, car, etc.)

Item	Cost
SUB-TOTAL your capital needs:	£

3.2.2 Capital needs for children living with you or provided for by you.

INCLUDE:
- Only those capital needs that are different to those of your household shown above

Item	Cost
SUB-TOTAL your children's capital needs:	£
TOTAL of ALL capital needs:	£ 0.00

21

4 Other Information

4.1 Details of any significant changes in your assets or income.

At both sections 4.1.1 and 4.1.2, INCLUDE:
- ALL assets held both within and outside England and Wales
- The disposal of any asset

4.1.1 Significant changes in assets or income during the LAST 12 months.

4.1.2 Significant changes in assets or income likely to occur during the NEXT 12 months.

4.2 Brief details of the standard of living enjoyed by you and your spouse/civil partner during the marriage/civil partnership.

22

4.3 Are there any particular contributions to the family property and assets or outgoings, or to family life, or the welfare of the family that have been made by you, your partner or anyone else that you think should be taken into account? If there are any such items, briefly describe the contribution and state the amount, when it was made and by whom.

INCLUDE:
- Contributions already made
- Contributions that will be made in the foreseeable future

4.4 Bad behaviour or conduct by the other party will only be taken into account in very exceptional circumstances when deciding how assets should be shared after divorce/dissolution. If you feel it should be taken into account in your case, identify the nature of the behaviour or conduct below.

4.5 Give details of any other circumstances that you consider could significantly affect the extent of the financial provision to be made by or for you or any child of the family.

INCLUDE (the following list is not exhaustive):
- Earning capacity
- Disability
- Inheritance prospects
- Redundancy
- Retirement
- Any plans to marry, form a civil partnership or cohabit
- Any contingent liabilities

4.6 If you have subsequently married or formed a civil partnership (or intend to) or are living with another person (or intend to), give brief details, so far as they are known to you, of his or her income, assets and liabilities.

Annual Income		Assets and Liabilities	
Nature of income	Value (if known, state whether gross or net))	Item	Value (if known)
Total income: £		Total assets/liabilities: £	

24

© Crown copyright

5 Order Sought

5.1 If you are able at this stage, specify what kind of orders you are asking the court to make. Even if you cannot be specific at this stage, if you are able to do so, indicate:

  a) If the family home is still owned, whether you are asking for it to be transferred to yourself or your spouse/civil partner or whether you are saying it should be sold

  b) Whether you consider this is a case for continuing spousal maintenance/maintenance for your civil partner or whether you see the case as being appropriate for a "clean break". (A 'clean break' means a settlement or order which provides amongst other things, that neither you nor your spouse/civil partner will have any further claim against the income or capital of the other party. A 'clean break' does not terminate the responsibility of a parent to a child.)

  c) Whether you are seeking a pension sharing or pension attachment order

  d) If you are seeking a transfer or settlement of any property or assets, identify the property or assets in question

5.2 If you are seeking a variation of an ante-nuptial or post-nuptial settlement or a relevant settlement made during, or in anticipation of, a civil partnership, identify the settlement, by whom it was made, its trustees and beneficiaries and state why you allege it is a settlement which the court can vary.

5.3 If you are seeking an avoidance of disposition order, or if you have already applied for such an order, identify the property to which the disposition relates and the person or body in whose favour the disposition is alleged to have been made.

25

© Crown copyright

Sworn confirmation of the information

I _____ *(the above-named Applicant/Respondent)*

of _____ MAKE OATH and confirm that the information given above is a full, frank, clear and accurate disclosure of my financial and other relevant circumstances.

Sworn by the above named

at)
)
)
)
this   day of   20   ) _____

Before me, _____

A solicitor, commissioner for oaths, an Officer of the Court appointed by the Judge to take affidavits, a notary or duly authorised official.

Address all communications to the Court Manager of the Court and quote the case number. If you do not quote this number, your correspondence may be returned.

26

Schedule of Documents to accompany Form E

The following list shows the documents you must attach to your Form E if applicable. You may attach other documents where it is necessary to explain or clarify any of the information that you give in the Form E.

Form E paragraph	Document	Please tick		
		Attached	Not applicable	To follow
1.14	**Application to vary an order**: if applicable, attach a copy of the relevant order.			
2.1	**Matrimonial home valuation**: a copy of any valuation relating to the matrimonial home that has been obtained in the last six months.			
2.1	**Matrimonial home mortgage(s)**: a recent mortgage statement in respect of each mortgage on the matrimonial home confirming the amount outstanding.			
2.2	**Any other property**: a copy of any valuations relating to each other property disclosed that has been obtained in the last six months.			
2.2	**Any other property**: a recent mortgage statement in respect of each mortgage on each other property disclosed confirming the amount outstanding.			
2.3	**Personal bank, building society and National Savings accounts**: copies of statements for the last 12 months for each account that has been held in the last twelve months, either in your own name or in which you have or have had any interest.			
2.4	**Other investments**: the latest statement or dividend counterfoil relating to each investment as disclosed in paragraph 2.4.			
2.5	**Life insurance (including endowment) policies**: a surrender valuation for each policy that has a surrender value as disclosed under paragraph 2.5.			
2.11	**Business interests**: a copy of the business accounts for the last two financial years for each business interest disclosed.			
2.11	**Business interests**: any documentation that is available to confirm the estimate of the current value of the business, for example, a letter from an accountant or formal valuation if that has been obtained.			
2.13	**Pension rights**: a recent statement showing the cash equivalent transfer value (CETV) provided by the trustees or managers of each pension arrangement that you have disclosed (or, in the case of the additional state pension, a valuation of these rights). If not yet available, attach a copy of the letter sent to the pension company or administrators requesting the information.			
2.15	**Employment income**: your P60 for the last financial year in respect of each employment that you have.			
2.15	**Employment income**: your last three payslips in respect of each employment that you have.			
2.15	**Employment income**: your last form P11D if you have been issued with one.			
2.16	**Self-employment or partnership income**: a copy of your last tax assessment or if that is not available, a letter from your accountant confirming your tax liability.			
2.16	**Self-employment or partnership income**: if net income from the last financial year and the estimated income for the next twelve months is significantly different, a copy of the management accounts for the period since your last accounts.			
State relevant Form E paragraph	Description of other documents attached.			

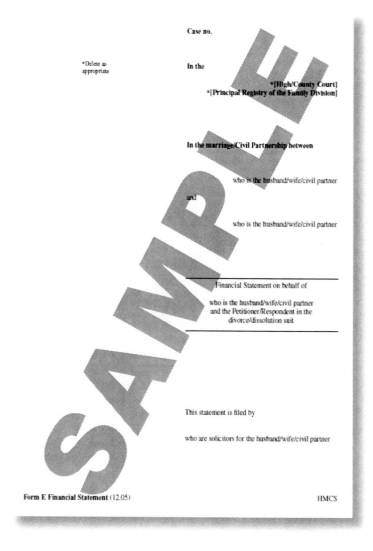

Resources

References

***Men are from Mars, Women are from Venus,* by John Gray (May 1992)**
Published by Harper Paperbacks, January 1st 2004 (first published 1992)

ISBN 0060574216 ISBN13: 9780060574215

Office of National Statistics
www.ons.gov.uk

BBC documentary, Who Needs Fathers? The Right to be a Dad (2010)

www.bbc.co.uk

HM Courts Service

For full information on HM courts service and forms
www.hmcs.gov.uk

Contacts

Resolution

Resolution's 5,500 members are family lawyers committed to the constructive resolution of family disputes.

www.resolution.org.uk

Surrey Family Mediation Service

They have been mediating in Surrey since 1981, one of the first such services in the UK.
Surrey Family Mediation are a not for profit service in the county. Other areas in the UK have their own regional mediation services.

www.sfms.org.uk

National Family Mediation

Mediation helps parents who live apart stay close to their children.

www.nfm.org.uk

Relate, The charity

Relate, The relationship people, which is a charity, offers advice, relationship counselling, sex therapy, workshops, mediation, consultations and support face-to-face, by phone and through the website.

www.relate.org.uk

Citizens Advice Bureau

Every Citizens Advice Bureau is a registered charity reliant on the commitment of trained volunteers and funds to provide vital services for local communities.

www.citizensadvice.org.uk

Family Mediation Council

The Family Mediation Council was set up with the aim of harmonising standards for family mediation. The founder members maintain registers of family mediator members who meet those standards.

www.familymediationcouncil.org.uk

For Independent Financial Advice

Churchouse Financial Planning Limited in Guildford, Surrey is a Chartered Financial Planners offering independent financial advice in divorce situations. Keith Churchouse is also an Accredited Financial Neutral by examination by Resolution.

www.churchouse.com

Child Support Agency

The agency's role is to make sure that parents who live apart from their children contribute financially to their upkeep by paying child maintenance.

www.csa.gov.uk

Also

Child Maintenance and Enforcement Commission

The Commission is a new Non-Departmental Public Body established to take responsibility for the child maintenance system in Great Britain.

www.childmaintenance.org

The Legal Services Commission

For full details and conditions on the Legal Aid System and eligibility

www.legalservices.gov.uk

Direct Government Information

Details on public services, all in one place.

www.directgov.gov.uk

Also

The Department for Social Development (For Pension Tracing)

To help locate any pensions that may have been lost over time.

www.dsdni.gov.uk

The Pension Service

For information on State Pension Benefits, including details of estimated incomes, transfer values and dates when State Pension benefits will be available.

www.thepensionservice.gov.uk

HM Revenue & Customs (formerly the Inland Revenue)

For information on the taxation system, rules and collection of the UK

www.hmrc.gov.uk

About the author

Having worked in the financial services industry for a quarter of a century and qualified to a high level within UK retail financial services, Keith set up Churchouse Financial Planning Limited with Esther Dadswell in 2004.

A Chartered Financial Planning Company in Guildford, Surrey, the company offers independent bespoke advice to clients and enquirers. This ranges from pensions and retirement planning, including tax planning, through to investments, wealth management, business and health and life insurance protection planning.

Keith also completed a BA (Hons) degree in Financial Services in 2007 with Napier University and became a Fellow of the Personal Finance Society in December 2007. In 2008, using Standards International, he was the fourth person in the UK to achieve ISO 22222 Certified Financial Planner status, the British Standard for Personal Financial Planners.

Pensions in divorce have become one of Keith's specialisms. Divorced twice himself, he has some personal knowledge and experience of the overall process. In addition he is a Resolution-accredited Financial Neutral for the divorce process.

Keith detailed his 25 years experience in financial services by writing the book, *Sign Here, Here and Here!...Journey of a Financial Adviser.*

Churchouse Financial Planning Limited has been Highly Commended at the Gold Standards Awards in both 2007 and 2008.

He has made regular and significant press comment in the local and national press and has frequently been interviewed on the radio over the last five years.

Keith has an active social media presence and can be found on Linkedin.com and Twitter as 'onlinefinancial'.

In addition, he tries to have a life outside work, and enjoys writing books, art, keeping fit by cycling and exercise and scuba diving.

Bulk Order Form

Addicted to Wedding Cake, The Journey of Divorce

If you would like to place a bulk order (minimum 10 books) for this book then this can be achieved with a direct discount of 25% per book (plus postage and packaging).

Item	Each	Quantity	Amount
Addicted to Wedding Cake. . .	£9.75		
Postage (per 10 books)			**£15.00***
	Total	£	

Please make cheque and payments payable to:
**Churchouse Consultants LLP**

Your details:

Name :
Address :
Postcode :
Contact Number/Email :

Post your order to:
Hadleigh House, 232 High Street, Guildford, Surrey, GU1 3JF

Our contact details for further information:

Tel: _**01483 578800**_ Fax: 01483 578864
Email: _**info@churchouse.com**_
**www.addictedtoweddingcake.co.uk**

Addicted to Wedding Cake
Hadleigh House,
232 High Street,
Guildford,
Surrey,
GU1 3JF

Lightning Source UK Ltd.
Milton Keynes UK
27 June 2010

156156UK00001B/8/P